D1519434

The Bookseller's Apprentice

George Talbot Goodspeed

The
Bookseller's
Apprentice

by
George Talbot Goodspeed

Anything that's a book

HOLMES PUBLISHING COMPANY
Philadelphia
1996

Seven hundred and fifty copies of this book have been printed by
KNA Press, Inc.
107 North Union Street
Kennett Square, PA 19348

HOLMES PUBLISHING COMPANY
230 South Broad Street, Third Floor
Philadelphia, PA 19102
215/735-1083

Copyright © George T. Goodspeed 1996
Library of Congress Catalog Card Number 95-082039
ISBN 0-9619693-6-9

Contents

Illustrations

Publisher's Foreword

Anyone who has gone to Boston to look for rare books in this century will have memories of Goodspeed's Book Shop. The shop was founded in 1898 by Charles Eliot Goodspeed who recorded the story of the firm's early years in his book, *Yankee Bookseller*, published in 1937. During its long history, the book shop occupied a number of locations, beginning in a basement at 5A Park Street adjacent to Boston Common and, after existing at various sites on Beacon Hill, returning finally and fittingly to rooms upstairs at 9 Park Street, where it closed in February of 1995. From 1927 on, there was also an "Old South Branch" of Goodspeed's, a spacious underground book shop equipped to handle large libraries of good used books, in the basement of the Old South Meeting House at No. 2 Milk Street. Most of the rare material, however, was sold on the Hill.

My own memories of Goodspeed's are mostly from the years 1972 to 1975 when the main shop was at 18 Beacon Street, and I was starting a rare book business in the borderland between Boston's Back Bay and South End. It was an interesting time for antiquarian books in Boston, and there were numerous fellow booksellers to visit. On Kingston Street, there was Sam Morrill, the very likeable proprietor of Edward Morrill and Son at No. 25, and, further along at No. 37, the Starr Book Company, owned by Ernest Starr, where his son Norman and Peter Stern were then apprentices. George Gloss had, within recent memory, moved his Brattle Book Shop to No. 5 West Street, and his son Ken was then learning the trade. The Williams Book Store still had a residual stock, venerable Lauriat's retained a section of rare books in fine bindings, and Goodspeed's Old South Branch was flourishing under the guiding hand of Arnold Silverman.

Across the Charles River in Cambridge, Arthur Freeman, of Hoffman & Freeman, had opened an American branch of Quaritch. There was also Gordon Cairnie's mecca for poets, The Grolier Book Shop; another Starr Book Shop (this one run by Ernest Starr's brother, Milton); the Temple Bar Book Shop owned by James O'Neill, whose brother, Eugene, operated In Our Time Books; and Pangloss for scholarly books. But Goodspeed's was unquestionably the dominant firm on the scene. It's prominence, both locally and internationally, coupled with the fact that the shop, in good Yankee tradition, kept its secrets to itself, made Goodspeed's the subject of frequent rumors and speculations in the local trade, many of them unfounded and not all of them kind. Indeed, the shop, had a kind of mystique which lured me strongly, as it had countless others.

Whenever I felt shop-bound, I left my office, walked to Boylston Street, crossed the Public Gardens and climbed the Hill to Goodspeed's. There was always a feeling of excitement when I reached the corner of Park and Beacon Streets and saw the shop's sign, elegantly printed in black and gold with its famous logo depicting a horse and rider and the words "Anything that's a book" which hung above the door. With luck, the window displays on either side of this door would have been freshened up since my last visit to include new items from a recently acquired Old Bostonian library.

Upon entering the shop, one came into a large open room lined with bookshelves and glass-fronted bookcases which extended the length of the floor. In the center were various tables and cabinets for prints. A mezzanine ran along the sides and back, and here employees could be seen working at desks, while, immediately to the right, sat Mrs. Gerstein (Louisa Solano) and, later, Miss Shrigley, who directed customers to the appropriate departments. The print department was straight ahead. It was run by Mrs. Adams, whom I often saw there but with whom I never had occasion to speak. My interests lay in literary material and much of my time was spent on the right side of the first floor looking at first editions which were kept in glass cases which had to be opened by a key. This key unlocked a series of annoying ratchet locks which made a loud grating noise announcing one's presence and location to everyone else in the room. There were always surprises tucked among the stock inside these cases. Often there were leavings from previously purchased local libraries and important collections such as, in my time, the books from George E. Woodberry's library, Philo Calhoun's collection and Paul Seybolt's first books. Inside each book was a typed description, and, as I generally committed these descriptions to memory, they provided, over time, no small contribution to my education. But my goals weren't only educational. Like every scout who visited Goodspeed's, I always hoped that my arrival at the cases coincided with the shelving of new acquisitions, since books at Goodspeed's were modestly priced and often sold swiftly. I bought my first book as a new bookseller from one of these cases. It was a copy of Eden Phillpotts' best-known novel, *Children of the Mist,* for which I paid $7.50 and which I sold, not long afterwards, for $15.00. A great success!

After looking at the first editions, I climbed the recessed stairway to the right, passed the genealogy mezzanine where the genial Mr. Farquharson, Sr. was in charge, to reach the autograph department in a room directly at the top. Here were well-organized file cabinets of autographs neatly arranged beneath an array of framed pieces displayed on the wall above. Mr. Banks, then one of the elders on the staff (whom I only asked for a discount *once*) was in charge, assisted by Mrs. Rochefort who soon after his retirement took over the department. There was a great range of material in this autograph room, and interesting, reasonably priced, literary finds were commonplace. After this stop, I ventured further onto the upper floor to the Americana department where a friendly contemporary, Bailey Bishop, was newly in charge, having taken the baton over from the legendary Mr. Walsh who was still present on certain days, in a kind of semi-retired consultant capacity.

To a young non-New Englander, there was an appealing "Yankee" feeling about the shop, a kind of aloofness or reserve. It was a place where people were still called "Mr.", "Mrs", or "Miss", and certain matters of form were taken for granted. Discounts were not loosely given to the trade, and one had to earn a thirty day credit. (You were notified of this achievement by letter from the bookkeeping department.) As a matter of course, the shipping department was located somewhere out of sight. And there were the private areas to which only the privileged were invited. It was several months before I was shown into George Goodspeed's second floor office or permitted to view the treasures of the vault hidden beneath the stairs on the first floor.

Mr. Goodspeed was likely to appear on any floor or in any department at any moment. He was then in his seventies and had been working at the shop since 1924. In the frontispiece of this book, in a photograph taken much later in the 1990's, he looks much as I remember him in 1972. On average, I spent parts of two days at Goodspeed's every week, and took to going in early on Saturdays during the winter months, when the shop was open till noon and was surprisingly quiet, Mr. Goodspeed being there by himself or with just a skeleton crew. I always called him Mr. Goodspeed and he called me Mr. Holmes, despite the fact that I was a "youngster" in my twenties. (It was many years, long after I'd left Boston for Philadelphia, before we graduated to a first-name basis.) George's conversation during these Saturday visits was especially beneficial because, as he recounted his many experiences with such great collectors as Carroll Wilson, F. H. Day, Frank Hogan, etc., he was painting, for a young beginner, a picture of the rare book scene on a grand scale, not only in Boston but in the world at large. The publication of this book is a small repayment to George for the friendship he showed me during the early days of my career as well as a tribute to the shop during his tenure there.

The second chapter of this book, "The Bemis Leavings," was published in *The Book Collector* (Vol. 28, No. 3, pp. 401-410) for Autumn, 1979. In 1983, the first chapter appeared in the Antiquarian Booksellers Association of America's journal, *The Professional Rare Bookseller* (No. 5, pp. 3-18), a periodical of limited circulation, with the statement that these were "the heretofore unpublished opening chapters of George Goodspeed's autobiography." Then silence. On a visit to Goodspeed's, now located at 7 Beacon Street, in 1990, I asked George when we would see the rest of his memoirs. He replied that he had written a good deal more, but that it was still in typescript form, and he doubted whether it was publishable. I offered to read it with an eye to publication, if he had no one else in mind to do it. When I returned to Philadelphia, a package arrived containing the text of complete chapters and fragmentary pieces which George had written in the 1970's and early 1980's. As I read them, the book seemed to take shape, and I asked George if I could edit it to the extent of arranging the completed segments and chapters to make a book. He said I could, and I did so, sending him, not long afterwards, a copy of the text that more or less comprises this book.

Then George decided not to publish. Nearly four years passed before he called one day and said he had been re-reading the manuscript and it was "not as bad" as he'd remembered. I took the hint and arranged a visit with him. He was now living in retirement in an apartment on Beacon Hill. This time he gave me his blessing. Readers will not find in the following pages a detailed history of Goodspeed's from the writing of *Yankee Bookseller* onwards, but rather a series of reflective pieces written by a central figure in the enterprise that was Goodspeed's after 1924. In addition there are three appended pieces, two published in Goodspeed's catalogues and one in *Antiquarian Bookman,* which seemed worthy of inclusion. In all, one gets a feeling for the shop and its founder's son, whose apprenticeship served him well as Boston's second generation Yankee bookseller.

David J. Holmes
Philadelphia, November 1995

COLLECTORS & BOOKSELLERS

I AM NOT unmindful that what I put down on the following pages overlaps to some extent what my father wrote in *Yankee Bookseller* many decades ago. But there are some matters which for obvious reasons he felt inappropriate to say at the time, and some which he left unsaid for reasons of modesty. What may be partly repetitious here represents a different point of view, at least, and there may be some justification in carrying on the history of what has been partly a family enterprise, for another generation.

C.E. Goodspeed's formal education was limited to what was available in the elementary schools of his youth; and though years later he became an honorary Master of Arts and a member of Phi Beta Kappa, he retained throughout life that inflated valuation of what is sometimes called "higher education" often held by those whose own education is self-acquired.

I was, accordingly, given the best education (it was believed) that circumstances afforded. Two years each at Roxbury Latin School and Exeter prepared me for admission to Harvard College, where partly from a false sense of values acquired at the second of those two preparatory schools, and partly from a lack of aptitude for the physical science, I pursued a somewhat less than distinguished academic career. Nevertheless, I emerged from Harvard in 1925 with a bachelor's degree. Such education as I gathered in the process may have been largely osmotic, but it proved helpful in later years.

An old salary book in the archives of Goodspeed's Book Shop

records under June 18, 1924 the employment of George T. Goodspeed at a weekly wage of fifteen dollars, but this was a summer job, and I was not permanently employed until Commencement Day, June 22, 1925. Besides myself, three other members of the Harvard class of 1925 at one time or another joined the staff of this rapidly expanding enterprise.

The first of these, Gordon Guptill, was brought in, I recall, by Louis Holman, head of our Print Department, who had known him as a boy in Needham and as a roommate of Holman's son, Richard. Gordon stayed with us for a year and a half, leaving at the end of that time, I imagine, under the impression that thirty-five dollars a week wasn't enough on which to support a wife.

The second of the three, Adrien Gambet, joined us in April, 1926 after six months at Harvard Divinity School. He was a picturesque character, vaguely resembling Mrs. Peterkin's son Agamemnon. He was shaped like a tooth-pick, with an Adam's apple more prominent than the chin above it, and a superior manner, heightened by a somewhat adenoidal style of speech. He was a good chess and bridge player, his intellectual equipment being well above the average. He was a competent cataloguer, but not easy to get on with. He took to ordering books from English booksellers for his personal library, using our letterhead, and on one occasion when we had to pay a bill which he had neglected to honor, he was outraged, complaining that we had interfered in his personal affairs. He left us after a year or so to form a partnership with Gordon Cairnie in the Grolier Book Shop, still located in Cambridge. (Its present proprietress, Ms. Louisa Solano, is also an alumna of Goodspeed's.)

The Grolier phase of Gambet's career was also short-lived, and he moved to New York, where the late Max Harzof got him a succession of jobs in the New York trade, all of equally brief duration. One of his employers was Gabriel Wells. Soon after Gambet went to work for him, G.W. took a trip to England. Francis Edwards, of London, was a passenger on the same boat. Edwards had with him a sheaf of bills which he had been unable to collect from his American customers. When Wells found the name of his new employee among them, he sent a radiogram to his shop, firing Gambet. I believe this is the only instance on record of a bookshop employee being discharged from the middle of the Atlantic. At one time or another, Gambet worked for Rosenbach, James F. Drake and Thomas F. Madigan. He died in 1948 having, I suppose, established some kind of record for the number of booksellers by whom he had been employed, though as early as 1931 he wrote that he had made "a graceful exit from a wretched business . . . in which the only one who has a chance of making a decent living is the man who owns the shop . . ."

A third classmate, Norman Dodge, who had been working for DeWolfe & Fiske a few doors below our Park Street shop, came to us in June, 1926, and upon Gambet's departure moved to the hill to Ashburton Place as cataloguer in the Americana Department. In the fall of 1929 under the inspiration of Louis Holman, he compiled the first number of a serialized catalogue which we called *The Month at Goodspeed's*. A gifted writer, Dodge had a delightful style somewhat like that of E.B. White. It was particularly suited to peddling our wares. The periodical became very popular with our customers, and despite C.E.G.'s fears that it might "peter out" it ran for four decades before publication was suspended in 1969. Its success was due to the great literary talent of the editor and the variety of material at his disposal. The compiler had complete freedom in the selection of contents, and the liberty (frequently exercised) of rejecting any item he thought unsuitable.

The business in 1925, was highly departmentalized, and if Goodspeed's is as we like to believe, *sui generis*, the fact is due to the ability of its founder to develop and hold specialists in several areas. When I came to work, Michael Walsh, probably the foremost Americanist in the trade, had already been with us sixteen years. It was under his tutelage that John Farquharson learned the highly specialized field of genealogy. When Guptill left us in 1927, the autograph and manuscript department, which until 1924 had been C.E.G.'s sole preserve, was put into the able hands of his son-in-law,

THE MONTH AT
GOODSPEED'S

Feb'y 1932

WASHINGTON   *Colored Mezzotint (p. 170)*

❀ BOSTON, MASS., U.S.A. ❀

An early issue of *The Month*, edited by Norman Dodge

Gordon Banks, under whom this seemingly limited specialty became one of the most active and profitable areas of our shop.

With us, as with many others, the late 'twenties were years of great expansion both of staff and premises. After the bankruptcy of the Williams Book Store in 1927, we bought its stock from the trustees and took over the lease together with Williams' assistant, Frances Egan, whose reputation as a searcher for out-of-print books is legendary. So, until the Park Street basement was abandoned in 1930, we had for a few years, three shops with more than sixty employees. There were six floor salesmen at Milk Street alone, and the Print Department under Louis Holman had a staff of eight.

With the closing of Park Street, Holman, with whom there had been an entirely amicable difference in policy matters, bought the bulk of our stock of small prints and went into business for himself in the old shop. He continued there until his death, when his son took over the print shop which, after numerous changes in location, survived until 1977.

Among the collectors who frequented our shop in those days were Frank Bemis, Percival Merritt and Harold Murdock, but of these it was only with Murdock that I had much to do. He was a daily visitor and I looked forward to his afternoon calls as a most agreeable part of the day's routine. But for the most part, these were customers of my father and it was not until Carroll Wilson came along that I had the satisfaction of following a collection almost from its inception.

Wilson became a customer of Goodspeed's in 1926, and for a few years he was our most consistent buyer of nineteenth century American literature. W.T.H. Howe of Cincinnati had succeeded Stephen H. Wakeman as the dominant collector in this field, but he was at that time the private preserve of Walter Hill of Chicago, and we knew him only by reputation.

A few years later, however, we ventured to offer Howe a copy of Poe's *Murders in the Rue Morgue* which, as a duplicate, had been placed in our hands for sale by the Huntington Library. The copy

5

wanted the wrappers, a near-fatal defect, since the pamphlet was issued without any title-page other than the front wrapper. However, rather to our surprise, Mr. Howe wired that he would like to see it. Could I call on him at the Commodore in New York the following Thursday? I could, indeed. This was before the days of air travel, and I went down on the morning train, arriving at three. Howe greeted me pleasantly enough, but hardly glanced at my book. It was evident that he had never had the slightest intention of buying it. He had merely wanted to ask me to offer him other things that might come along. I came back on the five o'clock, having spent two hours in New York without going outdoors.

Wilson was in some ways the greatest collector of American literature between Wakeman and Barrett and had a profound influence on everyone who knew him. My own friendship with him began on the day in 1927 when I found myself in New York on some excursion which had proven fruitless. Reluctant to come back to Boston without having made my expenses, I dropped in to call on Lathrop Harper. On his shelves were the privately printed issues of Holmes' *Fourth of July Oration* which Harper had bought three years earlier at the Wakeman sale. Knowing Wilson slightly as a Holmes collector, I took the books on approval, went into a phone booth and called him at his office. To ask for an appointment during business hours was, perhaps, presumptuous and I half expected a rebuff, but the answer was "I always have time to see booksellers." As general counsel to the Guggenheim brothers, he occupied a spacious office in the Equitable building, complete with secretary and assistant, but, while he was, as he put it, always on call, his employers' demands on his time were not heavy. My first visit, including lunch in the Bankers' Club on the top floor, ran to four hours.

The most enthusiastic bibliophile of his time, Wilson gave freely of his friendship to other collectors, booksellers and scholars and his influence on all of them was great. In later years I customarily used the spare bed in his Horatio Street penthouse as my New York lodging, and we became very close friends.

Having become a collector in 1925, he was just too late to have been a buyer in the Wakeman sale, and was a customer for such ephemeral pieces as had been sold in bundles at the time. P.K. Foley had bought many of these lots and I made a practice of dropping into his Hamilton Place office daily after lunch and picking at his stock, turning over the pickings to Wilson at a modest mark-up. Both P.K. and Carroll, of course, were aware of the process, which was agreeable to both of them, and for several years they dealt with each other, for the most part, through Goodspeed's.

My purchases from Foley on these visits were by no means entirely for Wilson, and since P.K. was kindly disposed toward me, week in and week out I brought the cream of the old gentleman's current purchases back to Ashburton Place. About this time, one or two of Foley's early customers were beginning to sell their collections back to him piecemeal, and some very attractive material turned up in this way.

One day Foley handed me a small sheaf of manuscripts. It consisted of correspondence between F.B. Sanborn and members of the Emerson family about Sanborn's courtship of Emerson's daughter Edith. Included were Sanborn's retained copies of his letters to Mrs. Emerson, Edith and Ralph Waldo, himself, but the star piece was a twelve page letter from R.W.E. in which he laid the suitor out in withering invective, referring to Sanborn's attitude as one of "squint suspicion!" I sent a copy of the correspondence to Bliss Perry, whose course on Emerson I had taken at college. Mr. Perry thought they ought not to be put on the market, but rather offered to the Emerson family. To me this smacked of blackmail, however, and I prevailed upon my father to buy the letters himself for his own library. When in 1937 my wife and I moved to Concord, he gave them to us as appropriate to our new home. Thus they escaped destruction in the fire which leveled my father's house at Shirley four years later.

P.K. used to say of Carroll Wilson that he got more fun out of his collection than anyone he had known. Books, were, indeed, Wilson's principal interest in life. Separated from his first wife, he lived for several years the life of a bachelor. The demands of his profession were not such as to challenge his brilliant mind, and he was not much interested in sports. His friends were almost exclusively drawn from the bookish world; of the occasional exception he was as likely as not to make a convert. His Williams College roommate, Philo Calhoun, was one of these.

Wilson, had he not turned to the law, would have made a very great bookseller, but while he may, on occasion, have acted as *marchand amateur* only once do I recall his having bought a book for resale. It was, I believe, about 1929 or 1930 that Tregaskis catalogued a copy of the first edition of Hoyle's *A Short Treatise on the Game of Whist*, together with other rare pamphlets by the same author. The price, I recall, was in the neighborhood of $300.00. Carroll cabled for the lot and got it. He tucked it away in a vault, remarking to me that someone would pay him a large profit when the time came.

It was two or three years later that a stranger came into our shop asking for books on whist. I said that we had none at the moment. "Nonsense" was the answer, "let me look about." Half an hour later, he came to my desk with a stack of books two feet high. "See," he remarked, " you have quite a few." They comprised dictionaries, novels, books on behavior, and such, each containing some reference to the game. Clearly he was collecting in depth as Folger did with Shakespeare, or Arents with tobacco. Wilson then owed us somewhat more than $3000, not an inconsiderable sum in 1933. It seemed possible that Hoyle's pamphlet might be the means of liquidating the account, at least in part. Wilson had been asking $2500 for the Hoyle, but was willing to give me a commission of $500.00. Our customer, though a medical man, was on salary and wanted somewhat more than two years to pay. These terms were rather too generous, but we wanted to get the Wilson account reduced, so I agreed. (Actually, it was nearly four years before we were paid.)

Wilson's collecting interests were not limited to the Americans. His Hardys and his Trollopes were famous and it amused him to point out to overnight guests that "I keep my Trollopes in the bed-

A Souvenir

OF A SMALL GATHERING AT

2 HORATIO STREET

NEW YORK CITY

ON FEBRUARY 8, 1935

IN HONOR OF THE WINNER OF

THE NOBEL PRIZE

FOR WRITTEN UNDERSTATEMENT

Mr. John Carter

OF LONDON

"His reticence....is perfectly exasperating."
J.C.: *Binding Variants*, 1932, p. 27.

"Where ignorance is bliss,
'Tis folly to be wise."

9

room" where, indeed, the works of the great Victorian were shelved. A common interest in Trollope led to friendship with the great Trollopean, Michael Sadleir, a Director of the London publishing house of Constable & Company.

It was Constable who published Carter and Pollard's *Enquiry into the Nature of Certain Nineteenth Century Pamphlets*. In 1935, when the *Enquiry* had just been published, Sadleir and Carter visited New York, where John was to address the Grolier Club. In honor of this visit, Wilson organized one of his famous "small gatherings." This was held in his Horatio Street penthouse, and the gathered included, besides himself and the two transatlantic visitors, John Winterich, David Randall, Philip Blackburn and myself. Wilson had prepared a handsomely printed keepsake of the occasion for which he had culled an appropriate sentence from the bibliographical writings of each of the participants. I remain today the only survivor of this memorable occasion. Blackburn, by the way, was briefly associated with Goodspeed's as a cataloguer. He left us to study for the Episcopal priesthood, joining the order of the Holy Cross after ordination. Except for a brief interlude in the freight business, he remained a member of the order until his death in 1964.

Wilson died in 1947 leaving behind him one of those bad wills that only a lawyer writing his own is likely to perpetrate. Under its terms, I was left a legacy of $1500. The executors were requested (though not required) to get my written approval of any action they might take in selling the books and manuscripts in his library. If they were sold with my approval, the beneficiaries under the will were barred from making any claims against the executors on account of the manner in which the sale was made. I, in turn, was not permitted to buy the collection or any part of it.

The will expressly authorized the executors to pay me "reasonable fees and expenses" for my advice "in addition to the legacy bequeathed" to me. As far as I recall I was never asked nor, indeed, was I offered, any compensation other than the legacy, and as I look back, the estate got excellent value! Philo Calhoun (with Wilson's widow) was co-executor under the will, and it was in the course of settling the estate that Philo and I became close friends. The benefits of this friendship were not wholly intangible, for after Philo's death, a substantial part of his library was sold to Goodspeed's.

On my visits to P.K. Foley, I frequently encountered another of our customers, the late D.E. Kennedy, whose lanky frame was a familiar sight in the many book shops then surviving in Boston. There must have been seasons when he appeared without one, but I remember him always to be wearing a long top-coat. A felt hat sat squarely above an aquiline face whence protruded a long cigar, held like a bowsprit firmly between the front teeth. He had a sardonic sense of humor and tended to be rather secretive about his extensive collection, which he rarely let anyone see. He and Mr. Murdock were neighbors in Chestnut Hill, and they often encountered each other in our shop, but rarely, if ever, spoke to each other.

Of independent means and a great reader, Kennedy spent much of his time going the rounds of the trade. He had a rare book instinct that told him just where a new lot from a Back Bay house was being picked over by the bookseller who had acquired it and the uncanny knack of pulling out the best book in the pile, pressing the startled owner to price it then and there. The result, of course, was that he generally got a bargain.

It was on one of these visits that I showed him a recent acquisition of which I was very proud: a very fine copy of Charles Brockden Brown's rare novel, *Edgar Huntly*. I asked him seventy-five dollars for it, at which he took offense, indicating that I was trying to hold him up. Shortly afterwards I sold the book to Whitman Bennett at the same price, but Kennedy never entered our shop on the hill again, though he dropped in at Milk Street occasionally.

In his later years he began to dispose of his books, quoting them by mail to various members of the trade, particularly to the Seven Gables Bookshop, and when finally, after his death, the remainder of his library was sold to Harvard, it was stipulated that nothing might

131 **Whittier,** John G. Snow-bound. Port. 12°, ¼ mor., g. e. Boston, 1866.
$30.00

.•. First edition. Autograph "JOHN G. WHITTIER 28TH 2ND MO, 1866" followed by inscription — "*James M. Bugbee, with the love of* T. B. ALDRICH *Xmas 1871*," on fly-leaf.

132 **Williams,** Samuel. The natural and civil history of Vermont. Folding map. 8°, sheep. Walpole, N. H., 1794. $15.00

.•. Interesting association copy bearing an early inscription in the hand of Whittier—"*John Plummer from his friend* JNO. G. WHITTIER."

133 **(Woodworth,** Samuel). An excursion of the dog-cart. A poem. By an imprisoned debtor. 8°, stitched. N. Y., printed and published by William Bonker, Junior, No. 25 Terrier-Court, sign of the Greyhound, 1822. $15.00

Attributed to Woodworth on authority of an old ms. note on title-page. Not mentioned by Wegelin.

BOOKS FROM THE LIBRARY OF

JAMES RUSSELL LOWELL

The section of this Catalogue which follows, comprises books from Lowell's library at Elmwood, Cambridge, all containing his autograph and in many cases extensively annotated by him,

134 **Ariosto.** Orlando Innamorato di Bojardo : Orlando Furioso di Ariosto : with an essay on the romantic narrative poetry of the Italians ; memoirs and notes by Antonio Panizzi. 12°, ½ roan (bindings a little rubbed), 7 vols. London, William Pickering, 1830. $35.00

Autograph, "J. R. LOWELL" on half-title to each volume.

135 **Beauties** of England and Wales. By J. Britton, E. W. Braylay and others. Copper-plates. 12°, 26 vols., old ½ calf. London, 1801-16. $40.00

.•. Autograph of J. R. LOWELL inside cover of each volume. Bindings in poor condition, some covers broken at joints and strips of some of the backs missing.

136 **Blanc,** Dr. L. G. Grammatik der Italiänischen Sprache. 8°, ½ mor. Halle, 1844. $6.00

Autograph, "J. R. LOWELL, 1857," inside cover.

137 **Calderon.** Love, the greatest enchantment : The sorceries of sin : The devotion of the cross. From the Spanish of Calderon. Attempted strictly in English asonante and other imitative verse, by Denis Florence MacCarthy. Sm. 4°, clo. London, 1861. $15.00

Autograph, "J. R. LOWELL, Elmwood, 1861" on fly-leaf and note by him on margin of one page.

be sold to Goodspeed's. Whether this stipulation arose from our differences over *Edgar Huntly*, I do not know.

P.D. Howe, who began his collection in the early 'thirties, became Wilson's first serious competitor in the American field. No relation of W.T.H. Howe and a very different personality, he had inherited a modest collection of Whittier first editions from his father. This he proceeded to fill out, at the same time accumulating a comprehensive library of New England authors, including, besides the Wakeman writers, the later poets—Emily Dickinson, E.A. Robinson and Robert Frost, as well as a number of the earlier writers, notably Melville, not collected by Wakeman. He was almost from the beginning a customer of P.K. Foley also, but the greater part of his library had come through Goodspeed's, though he later became a steady buyer at Seven Gables and Scribner's. Through me he met Wilson. While their rivalry in the book market remained active throughout the rest of Wilson's life, it was a very friendly one, to the extent that in his will Wilson bequeathed to Howe the choice of five books from his Whittier collection.

One of Howe's authors was James Russell Lowell. Lowell's library was divided up among various members of his family and several large segments came our way at one time or another. They included many presentation copies from Lowell's contemporaries, including Holmes, Emerson, Longfellow and others. I recall particularly a copy of the first edition of Aldrich's *Story of a Bad Boy* with the charming pencilled inscription in the author's hand: "A Very Humble Little Book for Mr. Lowell."

Lowell's library was a very large one. He fancied himself a bibliophile, but on the whole his collection was rather that of a reader. He had nevertheless some taste for old books, which he annotated with notes of their rarity and significance. One such was an edition of Homer printed at Basle in 1551. He had acquired this handsome folio in the spring of 1839 shortly before he met Maria White, to whom he was married five years later.

Looking through the early chapters of Scudder's biography of

Lowell to see whether there was any mention of the copy of Homer, I came upon this passage in a letter dated June 13, 1840: "She [Maria White] is a glorious girl with her spirit eyes. On the mantel is a moss rose she gave me which when it withers I shall enshrine in my Homer . . ." I turned back to the old folio and found the rose, after a century, still there pressed between the leaves. A charming miracle of survival, it still remains there.

Lowell, by the way, comes into my father's story too. Only two or three years ago, there was brought to me this note on the letter-head of the Legation of the United States, London:

24th Jul, 1881

My dear Young Friend,

I can't send you the Queen's autograph & cannot ask for it with propriety; so I must needs disappoint you with mine.
Faithfully yours
J.R. Lowell
Master Charles E. Goodspeed

I note that this letter is dated barely a month after Master Charles Goodspeed's graduation from elementary school in Newton. His collecting instinct developed very early indeed!

Wilson having been first in the field, it was natural for us to feel that he was entitled to the first crack at desirable pieces, but his resources at this time were comparatively limited. He was realist enough to know that this placed him at some disadvantage, and took it in grace when an occasional prize was awarded to Howe, the man with the ready money. Nevertheless, there were times when we had to decide, arbitrarily, as to which of the two was to be offered a particularly desirable object. I like to think we were sufficiently diplomatic in handling such situations. At any rate, I remained friendly with both gentlemen.

Shortly after Wilson's death his collections were sold by Dave Randall at Scribner's. With the great Barrett collection at the

University of Virginia, the Howe collection remained the greatest library of New England authors in private ownership (subsequently, it was acquired by the University of Florida in Gainesville).

J.K. Lilly paid us his first visit in the late summer of 1927. His purchases on that occasion were modest, but a year later he bought freely, taking off with him the second copy of *Tamerlane* to pass through our hands, and his bill on that day was the largest we had yet rendered for a single transaction. Thereafter, for a dozen years or more he appeared in late August or early September on his way from his summer place on Cape Cod to his home in Indianapolis. Since the day of his arrival was unpredictable, we dared not be away from the shop until it had taken place. These visits usually included a ceremonial luncheon at the Parker House with the top of our staff, after which he visited our various departments to look over what had been laid out for him. He remained our customer until he stopped collecting, though as his interests changed from literature to science we had little for him. Among his last purchases from us were juvenile rarities: a very fine copy of *Peter Parley's Tales about America*, 1827, the first of the Peter Parley books, and then one of two known copies, and John Cotton's *Milk for Babes. Drawn out of the Breasts of both Testaments . . . for the Spirituall nourishment of Boston Babes in Either England* (London, 1646), also one of two known complete copies. Properly called the first American juvenile, this had slipped through the Harmsworth sale at Sotheby's inadequately catalogued, at a very low figure.

In this era it was fashionable for bibliophiles to compile lists of "highspots" and "hundred best" books in various fields, inspired, I suppose, by the Grolier Club's 1902 Exhibition of *One Hundred Famous Books in English Literature*. This list did not pretend to be selected for fame or quality in the absolute sense, but was based on what the exhibitions committee had been able to round up from the collections of the Club's members. Had its compilers dreamed that it might later become a canon of desiderata for biliophiles, I have no doubt they would have been amused. Lilly and many collectors of greater or lesser imagination than himself used this and similar lists as guidelines in building their collections. So, A. Edward Newton's list of "one hundred good novels," the Grolier's own *One Hundred Influential American Books* (1947) and *One Hundred Books Famous in Science* (1964) gave book buyers with limited imaginations charts to follow.

Lilly, though he clung to these guidelines, was willing to chart new courses, but for the most part they must be courses. And he was practical enough to sense that it was better to put the whole of any project into the exclusive hands of one bookseller. When he decided (rightly) that a collection of sheet music of Jerome Kern would be a significant contribution to the cultural history of America, he turned the entire buying of it over to us, without restriction. Naturally, the amounts involved were very small, but I fancy that the result more than justified the modest outlay.

Late in life, having given up collecting rare books, he became interested in the literature of the sea and, with the aid of consultants (including ourselves), compiled a list of books in this field. No longer a bibliophile, he was now interested only in texts and paid us to run periodic advertisements in *The Antiquarian Bookman* for his *lacunae*, which we were able to fill with some degree of success.

During Lilly's most active years as a collector, his library was housed in a building constructed for the purpose on the banks of Eagle Creek some nine miles outside of Indianapolis. Great pains had gone into the details of its construction. The exterior was faced with logs keeping with the tradition of the region, and while the interior fittings were as fireproof as was feasible, the metal furnishings, even to the telephones, were painted to simulate pine panelling. Heat was supplied by underground pipes so that the oil tanks and boilers were separated from the library building, thus minimizing the danger of fire. Living and eating quarters were in a separate building.

On my first visit to Indianapolis, we had a luncheon at Oldfields, his mansion in Indianapolis. We were to dine at the library and Lilly invited his wife to join us. "You understand," she said to me, "that while you are here, you are my guest. At the library we are both Joe's guests."

A wing at Eagle Creek contained stacks for the less valuable books. On this or another occasion, he took me into this section and remarked "here are five thousand volumes which cost me about ten dollars apiece. What are they worth wholesale?" I replied that the wholesale value of a ten dollar book was nominal. "My opinion also," he said.

He was not always as realistic. On one visit to Indianapolis, I showed him a fine copy of *Leaves of Grass* for which I asked $3000. He produced a slightly inferior copy which he had bought from the Drakes a year or two before. "I paid $4000 for this copy. Do you think it proper to return it?" I said that was up to the Drakes, but that the sale had been in good faith and I saw no reason why they should take the book back. When I got home I wrote suggesting that he buy my copy, and that I take his reject on sale. I have forgotten the exact terms proposed, but I recall that I concluded my letter "Let me know what you think of this proposition." The answer was prompt and concise: "You ask what I think of your proposal. I don't think very much of it. Yours sincerely."

After the library was moved to its new home on the Indiana University campus at Bloomington, Lilly gave Eagle Crest, including the 3500 acres surrounding it to Purdue University, which institution subsequently sold the property to the city of Indianapolis. It is now a park, believed to be the largest municipal park in the country.

I saw relatively little of Lilly during his last years. We had been and remained on friendly terms for a quarter of a century, but I was never able to penetrate his reserve. For a man of his background this is perhaps not remarkable.

1931, which I think of as the first of the depression years, found us dangerously over-staffed and but for an extraordinary windfall we should have operated at a loss for the first time in many years.

The fourteenth of February of that year, an imposing couple appeared at Ashburton Place, demanding to see the proprietor. The

17

identity of the strangers was soon disclosed. Mr. and Mrs. John Barry Ryan were the son and daughter-in-law of the recently deceased financier and street railway magnate, Thomas Fortune Ryan, who had amassed a fortune estimated at more than fifty million dollars, not an impressive fortune in these days but, it was, in its own day, one of the world's greatest.

Under the elder Ryan's will, the bulk of his fortune went into a spendthrift trust under which his favorite son John Barry was the sole beneficiary. Having lived for years on a modest allowance, the son found himself with an income of a million and a half dollars a year—sufficient, one might imagine, to give ample scope for indulging a taste for the better things in life.

Ryan's first purchase from us was an impression of Revere's engraving of the Boston Massacre, not then nearly as expensive a print as it is today. To be accurate, it was billed to Mrs. Ryan, and I imagine that, in view of the day, it was a Valentine gift from her to her husband. Two days later he bought a group of books from the library of Sidney L. Smith, the engraver, some with Smith's etched book-plate, and a dozen or more with original drawings used by Smith as book-plates.

For the rest of the year Ryan visited us three or four times a month, leaving a substantial order each time. He invariably popped in unannounced, and that we should not be unprepared, one of the young women on our staff, who commuted from her home by way of the South Station, was told to look at Track One, where the private car on which the Ryans always came to Boston was usually to be found.

Ryan was a compulsive spender rather than a collector. He bought largely on impulse and rarely with judgement, but it was inevitable that he picked up many choice things along the way. On one day in March, along with a fine lot of natural history, he bought a fine copy of the first edition of *Walden* and a copy of Thoreau's *Cape Cod* in literally new condition, so fresh that it might have been kept in cotton batting from the day of publication. This latter he determined to have put in a sumptuous binding by Sangorski and Sutcliffe, for which the binder was instructed to submit drawings for Ryan's approval. I remonstrated with him, suggesting that a less brilliant copy would do equally well for rebinding, but he was adamant, since he wished the original cloth covers to be bound in at the end, and it was essential that they be pristine. I have always regretted being a party to this desecration.

In October, we held an exhibition in our gallery of watercolors by Louis Agassiz Fuertes. The Ryans came in shortly after the drawings had been hung on the wall, and went through the show at top speed, gobbling up nineteen of them, comprising nearly half the collection. Fuertes' widow, who had consigned the pictures to us, was appalled, and withdrew the remainder from sale.

Among wholesale commissions from this Crocsus were the gathering of a comprehensive collection of books on bookplates, the duplication of our rather extensive art reference library, and as far as possible a complete collection of books printed by D.B. Updike at the Merrymount Press.

As the Christmas season drew near, Lippincott brought out an edition of Moore's *Visit from St. Nicholas* with illustrations in color by Arthur Rackham. Ryan was immediately taken with the book, and proposed to use it for his Christmas card. That it should be his and his only, he instructed us to buy up the whole edition, or all the copies still in the hands of the publisher, and to negotiate for control of the copyright. This was clearly impossible, but we were able to buy the remaining 3796 copies, and to purchase by wire many copies of the limited edition already in the trade. Our staff artist was commissioned to draw up a shipping label appropriate to the season, as well as a greeting card for enclosure. 1000 copies were boxed and labeled for mailing. Ryan brought us a copy of the New York Social Register with the names of his friends checked off, together with a supplementary list of friends not in Manhattan, and we mailed out 458 copies by first class mail, special delivery. I recall that one of the large paper copies was sent off to Pope Pius XI, of whom Ryan was a great admirer. Our bill for this operation amounted to $438.34, not including, of course, the cost of the books themselves. We had driven what we thought a hard bargain with the publisher, who invoiced the books at seventy-five cents a copy, on which we charged our customer a commission of 15 per cent.

Ryan was a man of vast, if sometimes misdirected, energy and was constantly coming to us with some new project. He fancied himself an amateur composer and had written a song in honor of his son, which he wanted published. But it must first be orchestrated. Would we engage Serge Koussevitsky to undertake the task? We dissuaded him but, with the help of Dorothy Adlow, music critic for the *Christian Science Monitor*, we were able to engage her future husband, the no less distinguished Nicholas Slonimsky. The song, thus prepared for the public, was copyrighted and issued by the Barry Vail Corporation, a firm set up by Ryan to handle his various publishing ventures. His most ambitious publication was *Pius XI on Christian Marriage*, printed by D.B. Updike. 1000 copies were printed on facing pages, the Latin text in roman, the English translation in italic. The italic being more compact, it was thus possible to make the concise Latin and the longer English texts come out evenly. Updike considered this one of his major accomplishments. 580 copies were offered for sale at fifty dollars a copy, and if I recall correctly, we sold a number to collectors of Updike's work. There was, in addition, a cheap edition of the English text, also printed by Updike, of 25,000 copies. Another Barry Vail publication was a reprint of a comic backgammon, copies of which he ordered from us on occasion. In effect, of course, he was buying these from himself, using us as agent. I recall also an edition of "Barry Vail's" *Verses* which we supplied to him in the same roundabout manner. I suppose he flattered himself that he was contributing to the success of his publishing house.

All of this was most rewarding on paper but by October Ryan had run up a debit balance of $26,000 on our books, after payments of under $9000 on account, and our bank was unimpressed with receivables as collateral. In October and November, Ryan gave us three notes totalling $25,000 which we discounted at the bank, our partners (and later directors) being required to endorse the notes personally. The first of these two was due on April 10th.

We were not, naturally, Ryan's only creditor. In addition to his New York town house, he maintained a suite at the Ritz Carlton which he had completely redecorated as well as a suite at the Piping Rock Club on Long Island. He bought an estate at Prides Crossing, and, as a gift to Mrs. Ryan, a country house in Stockbridge, Massachusetts. He was a substantial customer of Tiffany in New York, and through his publishing enterprise owed the Merrymount Press a matter of $15,000 or so. The first inkling we had as to the gravity of the situation came when my father, on a trip to New York, learned that a note given to the Scribner Bookstore had not been met. Incredible as it seemed, Ryan, with an annual income of a million and a half, was insolvent, and under the terms of the spendthrift trust, neither the principal nor his future income could be touched either by him or his creditors. And, were he to die, there was no assurance that there would be enough to pay his bills. In the meantime, his account with us had been going up steadily so that when the blow fell he owed us about $48,000.

Of course, when the situation became known, all of his creditors descended on him; but he had no liquid assets. In the financial climate of 1932 one could not afford to be too particular about the amenities. Since our notes had been discounted at the bank, we asked the bank's attorneys to bring suit, keeping us out of the proceedings as much as possible. Ryan, it appeared, was as nearly judgement proof as a man of his wealth could be. His estate at Prides was heavily mortgaged and his books, jewelry and polo ponies could hardly be turned into cash. I remembered, however, about the Stockbridge estate, and it occurred to me that, as a gift to his wife, it might be unencumbered, and that he might have neglected to have the title transferred to her. This turned out to be the case, and, under Massachusetts law, it was a simple matter to make an attachment, which was enough to protect our interest. Eventually we were able to

21

collect the whole debt, with interest and a third of our attorney's fees. Mr. Ryan never forgave us for attaching the estate, but as I have said, those were not times when one could afford to be too nice about such matters.

Ryan died in the spring of 1942 and in October of that year Parke-Bernet held an auction of *Americana, First Editions, Standard Sets, French Illustrated Books, Ornithological and Costume Books, the Library of a deceased Gentleman.* In the depressed market of 1942 the badly catalogued library realized a small portion of its cost.

I imagine that Ryan's selection of the Merrymount Press as the printer of his edition of *Pius XI on Christian Marriage* was at our suggestion, as the preeminence of D.B. Updike and his Merrymount Press was never called into question at Goodspeed's. It was accepted as a matter of simple fact. Most of the publications issued under the Goodspeed imprint came from Merrymount, the few exceptions being usually dictated by budgetary considerations. As time went on, much of our job printing was done there also, and from 1938 to 1948 *The Month at Goodspeed's* bore its imprint.

The last of our special publications in which Updike, himself, had a hand was a handsome broadside edition of the *Oath of Hippocrates* which we offered for sale in *The Month* for December, 1941. I think it must have been one of the last productions of the Press designed by him, as he died on the 29th day of that December. The January *Month* opened with a brief tribute by C.E. Goodspeed to Updike's memory.

The choice of text for the broadside presented problems, but I settled on the familiar translation of W.H.R. Jones, partly because other more authentic versions contained passages which might not be entirely acceptable to modern gynecologists. In my innocence, I had imagined that any physician would welcome this beautiful framing piece as a decoration for his office, and in our announcement of its publication we expressed "some fear that the limitation we have set on our edition will be too narrow and that the piece may go out of print disconcertingly soon." However, in spite of the modest price we put on it, the initial sale was not too large and even today two copies remain. Maybe doctors were sensitive about displaying such a set of rules on their office walls. The broadside, incidentally, is not to be found in the recently published supplement to the Merrymount Press bibliography.

After Updike's death, his partner, John Bianchi, continued the Press and our relations continued as before. Bianchi's son (and Updike's namesake) Daniel, who had been with the Press since his graduation from Harvard in 1926, entered the Navy in 1942. After his discharge in 1946, he returned to the Press.

In 1948 the loft building in Kenmore Square which had housed the Press since 1931 was sold. The Bianchis were faced with sharply increased rent, and as a result, liquidation of the business appeared imminent. Daniel Bianchi and I had become very friendly and I conceived the idea that Goodspeed's could buy the business and continue its operation under his direction. I felt that the volume of business might be built up to the point where it would sustain increased rent. I was probably wrong, and John Bianchi evidently thought so, for on January 31, 1949 formal announcement of the Press' closing was mailed to its customers.

I was greatly interested in buying the Press' file of its own printings. Bianchi, however, feared that were I to do so, they might wind up in hands he thought unfriendly. He accordingly sent the whole lot out to Huntington, where Max Farrand's Merrymount collection already reposed.

Many years before, my father and Updike had projected an edition of Jane Austen's works. The subscribers were few, however, and the project was abandoned. Updike had made two dummies for the proposed edition. These were among the file copies. One of them had the title-page; the other had no title, but a quire of text. I had mentioned my sentimental interest in them because my father's name appeared on the title as publisher. Bianchi, with kindly intent, sent me one of the two. Unhappily, it was the one without the title-page. The copy I had wanted had gone to the Huntington with the others!

23

PROPOSALS FOR THE PUBLICATION OF THE WORKS OF JANE AUSTEN. MERRYMOUNT EDITION. IN SIXTEEN VOLUMES, 16MO

MR. Charles E. Goodspeed and Mr. D. B. Updike submit herewith proposals for the publication of THE WORKS OF JANE AUSTEN, MERRYMOUNT EDITION, to be issued in Sixteen Volumes, 16mo, of about 346 pages each.

List of Volumes
- SENSE AND SENSIBILITY. *In three volumes.*
- PRIDE AND PREJUDICE. *In three volumes.*
- MANSFIELD PARK. *In three volumes.*
- EMMA. *In three volumes.*
- NORTHANGER ABBEY / LADY SUSAN } *In two volumes.*
- PERSUASION / THE WATSONS } *In two volumes*

In publishing and printing the Works of Jane Austen in this form, Mr. Goodspeed, as a publisher, and Mr. Updike, as a printer, are carrying out a wish which they have shared for a long time—namely, to produce an ideally readable and convenient edition, which shall be the standard for time to come. There is no really good edition of Miss Austen's books in a convenient form; the volumes of small, convenient format being printed in type of a size too small to be agreeable to the eye; and the editions of larger form and type being inconvenient and heavy to the hand.

It is proposed in the Merrymount Edition to return to the general form in which Miss Austen's Novels were originally published; issuing the longer novels in three volumes and the shorter stories in two volumes each. The print will be large and readable, the paper light, and the binding simple but appropriate. Thus this edition will reproduce the sort of book Miss Austen herself knew, without making it, however, a slavish imitation of the very imperfect printing of that date. *A special feature will be* THE RESTORATION OF THE ORIGINAL TEXT, *avoiding the numerous errors which disfigure most of the modern editions.* The price of the set of sixteen volumes will be $25.00.

If a sufficient number of replies is received to the proposals which are here made, the edition will be issued. If not, the project will be abandoned. It is hoped that the lovers of Jane Austen's novels—and they are many—will welcome the present proposal for a simple, straightforward, readable set of books which—like the author herself—shall be full of "sense" and "sensibility."

An immediate response from intending subscribers is earnestly desired.

When the Press was dismantled we did acquire the show-case in which samples of the Press' work had been displayed. Another souvenir of the press was a framed Caxton leaf which used to hang on the office wall. A portion of the leaf is reproduced in Updike's *Printing Types* above the caption "Caxton Type 2. From the *Dictes or Sayengis of the Philosophres*. Westminster, 1477. First book printed in England with date and place of printing."

I bought the leaf from Mr. Bianchi after the premises had been closed up. Neither he nor Updike (nor I at the time) realized that the caption (which still stands in the current edition) is correct only in the identification of the type. It is not from the *Dictes*, but from the *Canterbury Tales* of the following year.

A few years later, after John Bianchi died, Dan sold me the books in the cellar of the family home. There was a large quantity of over-runs of books printed at the Press and one that had been retained from the set of file copies. It was the history of the Scroll and Key Society at Yale, of which five copies were printed in 1942. Bianchi was concerned that this copy be disposed of with discretion, in view of the arcane nature of the book's contents.

As chance would have it, Lefty Lewis made one of his rare visits to the shop a few days later. "Are you not a member of Keys?" I inquired. When he answered in the affirmative, I handed him the book and told him the story of its provenance. It is now in the Society's archives.

During the half century of my working life, Goodspeed's retained the departmental structure which was evolving when I arrived on the scene. The structure was not planned but developed naturally as circumstances arose. Thus, there was no print department (the first specialized department) until Louis Holman arrived in 1922, no Americana department ("Americana" as the term is usually employed in the trade, as a term applied to *books* relating to the political, military and economic history of America; it does not include literary, autographic or pictorial material) until Michael Walsh returned to Goodspeed's after World War I and a year of convalescence from tuberculosis; no genealogical department until John Farquharson, who had operated under the Americana roof, finished his apprenticeship and became a full fledged and independent administrator of that important part of our business; no autograph department until the advent of Gordon Banks in 1927.

These departments all represent aspects of the business in which the proprietor had achieved a considerable reputation; that he was willing and able to educate his assistants and encourage them to take responsibility made it possible to expand the business and to keep promising personnel.

This departmentalization, on the whole, worked very well. The feeling of individual responsibility on the part of the department heads was, I think, rewarding to them, and a spirit of rivalry between departments, so long as it remains friendly, does, indeed, tend to increase the overall volume of business. The customer, too, is made to feel that he is getting the benefit of skilled advice from the person with whom he deals.

There are, inevitably, gray areas in which even we, ourselves, sometimes think we lose our way, and there are inconsistencies hallowed by time, which our customers find hard to comprehend. Thus, a history of Connecticut printed in the eighteenth century will be called Americana, while one printed three decades later will be shelved in local history. A first octavo edition of Audubon's *Birds of America* will be in the catch-all "rare books" department, while Say's *Entomology* will be Americana. Maps from an atlas will be classified as prints, but a complete atlas may be Americana or (again, if early enough) "rare books." The poems of Anne Bradstreet will be Americana, as will separate poems by Philip Freneau, though Freneau's collected poems will be found among the section devoted to *belles lettres*. When is an American broadside, which features an engraving, a print and found in that department, or when is it called a broadside and found with Americana? Many of these anomalies must be resolved individually, and a spirit of give and take is required to avoid friction.

* * * * * * * * *

26

THE BEMIS LEAVINGS

PROBABLY the greatest book collector in Boston in this century was Frank B. Bemis whom I remember as a frequent caller at our shop and an old friend of my father's. His appearance was that of a typical State Street banker, ruddy-faced, with what we then called a Prussian haircut, and close-clipped moustache, wearing, in the appropriate season, the high-crowned derby and short gabardine coat or reefer affected by substantial Bostonians of the time. Despite his somewhat ponderous manner, he was a pleasant, friendly man who, though his book-buying was mostly done in the more elegant establishments of London and New York, consulted us often, and gave us occasional commissions. Though he was a substantial customer of Rosenbach, Quaritch, Pickering and other leaders in the trade, he was of a retiring disposition, and his collection was not widely known. But he had been, for a decade and a half, one of the two or three leading American collectors. Among his treasures were the unique copy of William Blake's *Milton*, containing a hitherto unknown leaf of poetry, which was the subject of a monograph by Foster Damon published by the Club of Odd Volumes in 1925; a very fine copy of the first folio Shakespeare in the original binding; the original manuscript of Keats's *Lamia*; a Poe collection that included *Tamerlane* and the original manuscript of "The Spectacles"; a fine copy in the original boards of Keats's *Poems*, inscribed to John Hamilton Reynolds; and the very rare first edition of Milton's *Comus*.

In 1924 Bemis had given the collection to his fellow O.V.'s Harold Murdock and John Woodbury, as trustees for the Children's

27

Boston Athenaeum
Portrait of Frank B. Bemis by Edmund Tarbell (1862-1938)
Oil on canvas, 1926

Hospital, for whose benefit it was to be sold after his death. The trust instrument executed by Bemis and the trustees in his library on 15 February stipulated that the books were to remain in the possession of the donor during his lifetime and that he be permitted to add to the collection or improve it by exchange as opportunity might arise.

Unhappily, Murdock predeceased Bemis by a year. He was one of Bemis's most intimate friends. A great bookman, conscientious and possessed of rare judgement, he was ideally qualified for the trust, and had he lived I believe the disposal of the collection would have been handled differently. After Murdock's death Bemis named Francis Hart, President of United Fruit and Vice-Chairman of the Old Colony Trust Company, to succeed him as co-trustee.

Bemis died in 1935, and the trustees were faced with the task of selling the collection. They not unnaturally turned to Rosenbach, from whom much of the library had come. The Doctor at this time was having his financial problems and being in no position to buy the collection himself, hardly relished seeing it sold elsewhere, by auction or otherwise. Accordingly he persuaded the trustees to place the books with him on consignment. The consignment, according to Rosenbach's biographers, was "on some basis keyed to the total cost of the collection to Bemis—just over $700,000." A memorandum left by Bemis notes that "Dr. Rosenbach stated to me on Oct. 26, 1932 that the books in the library were worth $3,000,000 *on that date*. An absurd statement but gives an idea of his estimate of their value. I believe them to be worth $1,000,000."

Hart died in 1938, to be succeeded in turn by Clarence Brigham, director of the American Antiquarian Society, who because of Woodbury's failing health became in effect the sole trustee.

The consignment seems to have been a wholly informal arrangement, with Dr. R. the umpire over his own operation. The attorney for the estate wrote to Brigham in April 1939, "There is one other matter that I think we may well take into account at the present time, *viz.* the compensation to be paid to Dr. Rosenbach. Mr. Woodbury seems a little indefinite about the arrangement made but has said something to the effect that he understood that Dr. Rosenbach is acting without pay . . ." He eventually paid the trustees about $400,000 for books that had cost Bemis $584,762. The procedure was very simple indeed. From time to time Rosenbach sent cheques to the trustees on account of books sold, listing the titles covered by each remittance. For example, in 1939 one payment of $15,000 was for the unbound copy of Gray's *Odes*, the manuscript of David Garrick's "To Mr. Gray on His Odes," Milton's *Paradise Lost, Paradise Regain'd* and *Poems* together with a presentation copy of *Evangeline* from Longfellow to Hawthorne; he had already sold the lot (without *Evangeline*) for more than $46,000, the Grays to Lord Rothschild, the Miltons to Frank Hogan.

John Woodbury died in 1939 and in January 1940 Brigham wrote to Rosenbach that "I shall not appoint a co-trustee" to which the Doctor replied "I am glad you have reached the decision not to appoint [one], as to my mind it was totally unnecessary. We can always work together." The authorities at the hospital were not happy with this arrangement, however: Samuel H. Wolcott, president of the Hospital trustees, suggested the appointment of Philip Hofer to the vacancy. Brigham, however, preferred someone closer at hand or possibly less independent, and in June he wrote to Edward L. Bigelow, the hospital treasurer, that he had appointed Theron J. Damon, a member of the Antiquarian Society and then on its staff as curator of manuscripts, to the post. Damon was never active in any way in the affairs of the trust. His name does not appear on the instrument, nor did he receive any compensation for his services. (It had been agreed that four per cent of the receipts was a reasonable fee, and the trustees had been paying themselves on that basis.) I question, indeed, whether the appointment was ever made, except *in pectore*.

In the meantime, however, payments from Rosenbach were becoming smaller and less frequent. Prodded perhaps by Hermann Clarke, by then treasurer of the Hospital, Brigham came to me in the Spring of 1944 with a list of books remaining in the collection. I estimated that they would be worth $125,000 to us, leaving out the four folios of Shakespeare, which were to be left with Rosenbach. The sum was agreed on as reasonable and I persuaded a skeptical banker to advance $100,000 towards the purchase price. Armed with this assurance, and with three index volumes of *American Book Prices Current* as my reference shelf, I went to New York on the 25th of July where I was to meet Brigham for breakfast the following morning. He had gone on ahead to check over the list.

He came into the dining-room of the Algonquin with a revised list of the books remaining. An appalling number of important items had been sold, but not accounted for. These included such star pieces as the presentation copy of Boswell's *Johnson*, *The Dictes or Sayengis of the Philosophhres*, printed by Caxton in 1477 and the first dated book printed in England; a *Pickwick* in parts; two manuscripts of Alexander Pope; the manuscript of Longfellow's *Hanging of the Crane* and of Kipling's *Recessional*, and a Grolier binding, to name a few, the total representing in Bemis's costs, a matter of $60,000. That the lot had shrunk so substantially was, of course, a great disappointment, many of the missing books being of exciting quality.

The next morning we took a cab to the Lincoln storage ware-house where the books were stored, and I went to work. At one point John Fleming appeared with a suitcase full of books which had been taken down to the Rosenbach shop. I spent all of that day and a fair part of the next revaluing the collection, for which I came up with an offer of $55,000. Brigham passed this figure on to Rosenbach, who insisted that it should be ten thousand more, to which after some argument in Brigham's hotel room, I finally agreed, and wrote out a check for ten thousand dollars on account. At no time during the proceedings did I see Rosenbach, everything being handled by Brigham. We had but two hours to go back to the warehouse where I could make arrangements to have the books packed, and catch our trains to Worcester and Boston respectively. I have forgotten just which books I crammed into my briefcase to bring back with me on the Merchants' Limited that evening, but I recall that a manuscript Book of Hours and, what was later to become the subject of much

controversy, the famous copy of *Adonais*, were among them. My ela-
tion was tinged with misgivings when I showed up at 18 Beacon
Street the next morning, having bought the most expensive lot the
house of Goodspeed had ever owned.

With the arrival of the shipment a few days later. I sent
Brigham the balance of $55,000, which he acknowledged as "the
largest check I have ever had payable to my order whether personal
or trustee." For reasons which are not clear to me, Rosenbach was
paid a commission of four per cent on the transaction. My purchase
price in relation to Bemis's costs was figured out at 29 per cent and
Rosenbach reimbursed the trust at about the same ration for books
he had sold but not reported. Nobody knows what he had got for
them!

In retrospect my purchase sounds like a bargain, and in today's
market it surely would be, representing as it did $225,000 in Bemis's
costs. However, there were minuses which soon began to appear. The
forgeries, of which there were a few, had naturally survived the stay at
Rosenbach's and had to be written off at once. And since Rosenbach
had wanted to make a reasonably good showing to the trustees, many
of the over-priced pieces also remained. Of American literature, with
which I was most familiar, and for which I had the readiest market,
very little was left. The statement had been made (Wolf and
Fleming, page 527) that "What was left was rich in special copies of
first editions by American authors." In fact, only ten thousand of the
two hundred and twenty-five thousand dollars represented American
books, and these, for the most part, were very ordinary indeed.

As I look over the list of my purchases, I remember with particular satisfaction such gems as the manuscript of Burns's "O, my luve's
like a red red rose" which J.K. Lilly got on his annual visit in
September 1944; the touching letter from Samuel Johnson to
"Dearest Tetty," the only surviving letter to his wife, which Donald
and Mary Hyde picked up on a visit to Boston the following May,
three years before they made the great Adam purchase; the *editio
princeps* of Thomas à Kempis's *De Imitatione Christi* 1473 bound with

ten other tracts, with the rare collective title, bought by W.K. Richardson and now at Harvard; the copy of Sir Thomas Browne's *Certain Miscellany Tracts* 1683, with frontispiece portrait in the first state and the autograph of the author's son; and the copy of *Adonais* with the autograph poem by Shelley.

Among the association copies in the lot were Addison's *Remarks on Several Parts of Italy* 1705, presented by Addison to his college roommate Henry Sacheverell, the copy of *Bells and Pomegranates* in the original parts, with inscription by Browning to his uncle Reuben; John Evelyn's *Ideas of the Perfection of Painting*, inscribed by him to Sir Peter Lely; and Rossetti's *Poems* 1870, inscribed to George Eliot.

There was very little of Dickens. An exception was a very fine copy of the third issue of *A Christmas Carol* 1843, inscribed on the half-title "Frederick Salmon Esquire from his friend Charles Dickens. Twenty-eighth March 1846." This was a highly appropriate book for the holiday trade and it was offered in *The Month at Goodspeed's* for December. It was, I think, the first Bemis book to find its way into any of our catalogues. It had come from the Kern sale, where it had realized $2500, and having regard for the decline of the market, we offered it at $1500. The lateness of the inscription hardly enhanced the book's value, but Salmon was Dickens's personal physician and the association was a desirable one. It was ordered by Colonel McKell of Chillicothe, Ohio, a great collector of children's books who, incidentally, was the purchaser a year later of the lovely 15th-century *Horae* in a Derome binding, also from the Bemis library. The colonel was a favourite customer for many years, a generous and discriminating buyer and a courtly gentleman. We were happy to see the *Carol* in such good hands and I think he was pleased with his purchase.

Years later, in 1951, we were called out to Topsfield to buy the fine library of botanical books left by Thomas Proctor. Among the miscellaneous books in the library was a small volume bound in green levant, lettered on the spine "A Christmas Carol. Dickens. Presentation copy to F. Salmon."

When this proved to be an uninscribed copy of the eleventh edition, 1846, it was obvious that the half-titles had been switched, so that the inscription from a re-bound copy of a late edition could be used to make a presentation first in original cloth. What enterprising faker was responsible, I never knew, though I have very strong suspicions. What I shall never understand is why he failed to destroy the re-bound copy, with the damning evidence on the backstrip.

I sent the mongrel copy to Colonel McKell with an explanatory letter, asking him to return the two copies so that I might refund the purchase price. He did so, in a gracious letter closing: "Your calling this to my attention when I would never have been suspicious after the sale to me by you in perfect faith just bears out the name which your house carries . . . I am returning the books as that is the suggestion which you make. Any adjustment which would lessen the loss to you would meet with my approval."

I sent him a refund cheque and, taking him at his word, proposed that I restore the two half-titles to their original volumes so that he would still have a valid presentation copy as well as a first edition in the original binding, and throw in a little lot of juveniles including a copy of *A Child's Garden of Verses* and some rare *New England Primers*.

Characteristically he wrote back that "I will be delighted to have the books and enclose my check for them . . . even the adventures of the Christmas Carol do not lessen its interest to me whatever it does to its sale value." Thus, what might have been a costly disappointment to me ended happily for both of us.

The most important and valuable book coming to us with the Bemis leavings was the famous copy of *Adonais* from the library of Richard Monckton Milnes with Shelley's poem "Remembrance" inscribed in his hand on the last two leaves. It had been sold in the Gaskell sale at Hodgson's on 28 February 1924. The first edition of Shelley's beautiful elegy on Keats, printed in Italy under the close supervision of the author has always been considered one of the great collector's pieces of the nineteenth century, and this copy with its distinguished provenance and the manuscript verses in Shelley's hand was held by Bemis to be one of the greatest treasures in his collection. It realized £2000 at the Gaskell sale and was bought by W.T. Spencer. Spencer must have been acting for Ned Bartlett of Boston, for Bemis's acquisition slip notes that the book was bought through Bartlett in London for £2200. In those days it was not customary for American booksellers to bid for themselves at London sales, and Bartlett seems to have used Spencer as his agent, though this seems a little surprising.

About this time, that is, 1944, the late Professor Robert Metcalf Smith of Lehigh University was conducting the researches into the forgeries of "Major" George Gordon Byron, which he published the following year under the title *The Shelley Legend*.

Unfortunately, Professor Smith, who had secured the services of a thoroughly competent handwriting expert, Louis A. Waters of Syracuse, was not content to pass judgement on the authenticity of such Shelley manuscripts as had been examined by Mr. Waters, but was rather free in casting suspicion on other things as well. Among these was the copy of *Adonais* which he had seen in the Rosenbach safe. Through David Randall, a former student, Smith met my friend Carroll Wilson, then at the height of his fame as a collector, and told him of his doubts about the book. On 21 September 1944, Carroll wrote to me:

> I have been giving a final reading tonight, against the fac-similes, of Professor Smith's paper on the Wise forged Shelley letters, and reflecting again on what he told me at the dinner which followed his reading it, and although it is none of my business, I am disturbed about the Bemis Shelley autograph material, including the poem in Adonais. He did tell me that a great deal of Pforzheimer and Rosenbach autograph material was the work of a forger, and of course he had access to the Bemis things when they were at Rosenbach's. You might want to let him

35

see the things before you make commitments about them. Certainly the forgeries are so good that (from the facsimiles) my untutored eye finds it very difficult to differentiate the true and the false.

I was not about to entrust judgement on so important a matter to a scholar whose qualifications were unknown, and as things turned out I was wise not to. In his recently published reminiscences, David Randall, in commenting on Smith's work, remarks: "Personally I will take any experienced dealer's autographic judgement on an author or a period he is familiar with, over that of a battery of handwriting experts or professional scholars," a sentiment with which I concur wholeheartedly. In any event, I think Carroll never entirely forgave me for not showing the book to Professor Smith, and thereafter he tended to throw cold water on the whole Bemis situation, writing me in December that "the bloom seems to me a little bit off the rose on the Bemis books." Unfortunately, he didn't live to hear the end of the story.

In November of the same year I made an appointment to show the *Adonais* to Carl Pforzheimer. On the way I stopped at Farmington to spend the night with Lefty Lewis.

In September, Lefty had bought, along with the second Bemis copy of Gray's *Odes*, and a third edition of the *Elegy*, the long Walpole letter to Gray about Bentley's *Designs for Six Poems by Mr. T. Gray*. Later when Lewis boasted to Rosenbach of this purchase, the Doctor remarked, "You should have bought it from me. I would have let you have it for less."

Bedtime is early at Farmington, and after dinner Lefty handed me the manuscript of his reminiscences, later published as *Collector's Progress*, suggesting that I use it for bed-time reading.

After retiring, my brief-case with *Adonais* at the foot of my bed, I started on the manuscript. Early on I was brought up with a start, as I came to the passage in which Lewis describes his first experience of a London book auction, the Milnes Gaskell sale in 1924:

36

This sale was memorable to me not only because it marked my first Walpolian purchases, but because of the presence at it of two persons, one of whom was Thomas J. Wise. He had come to see an uncut copy of *Adonais* sold . . . He beamed indulgently when *Adonais* was knocked down to [Spencer] for two thousand pounds, the highest price ever paid for a book at Hodgson's, as the auctioneer stopped the sale to announce.

Over breakfast the next morning I remarked to my host on the extraordinary coincidence that the same *Adonais* should have found lodging for the night at Farmington when I read the story.

When I called on Mr. Pforzheimer I was cordially received and treated to some pungent remarks about Professor Smith and his students, who had felt free to gossip about the authenticity of some of the letters in the Pforzheimer collection. He thought the stanzas in *Adonais* genuine, but it was evident that I couldn't use him as an authority.

In the meantime I was at work on a catalogue of the Bemis books, and at a loss as to how to treat *Adonais*. At this point, one of our associates, having done some research in the reproduction of the Shelley notebooks at Harvard edited by G.E. Woodberry and published by the John Barnard Associates in 1929, pointed out the remarkable similarity of the handwriting in our manuscript to some of Mrs. Shelley's in the notebook, notably in the poem "To-Night" on pages 69-70. This seemed the answer to the questions that had been raised, and in cataloguing the book we so attributed the manuscript, at a price considerably less than I previously had in mind.

Had I but left it out of the catalogue altogether! It developed that many of Woodberry's attributions were incorrect and the "To-Night" stanzas were indeed Shelley's, so we were back where we had started.

Having gone out on a limb, it was not easy to crawl back, but it had to be done. In February 1948 I wrote to Mr. Waters (Professor

Smith's expert) asking whether he would vet the manuscript for us. He agreed to do so on payment of $25.00 *in advance* "because . . . experience has taught me that some dealers are very reluctant to pay me for an adverse opinion." Agreeing to this very reasonable stipulation, I sent the book along with a cheque.

The poor man had made a bad bargain for himself, expecting to be able to send a brief negative verdict. Instead, finding the hand to be Shelley's and genuine, he was in for a full dress report, which authenticated it without qualification. His report, together with the *Adonais*, Shelley's *Address to the Irish People* and *A Proposal for putting Reform to the Vote throughout the Kingdom* went to Robert H. Taylor in July.

I recall one amusing aspect of this final transaction. Bob Taylor stipulated that I must dispose of the copy of *Adonais* already in his collection. "You should," he told me, "have no problem, for it is the Bandler copy which I bought from Charlie Boesen. I know that Brunschwig wanted it at the time I bought it, and would doubtless still take it."

I accordingly called on Dr. Brunschwig, an eminent European bibliophile then living in New York, who had been a customer of ours for several years. Yes indeed, he still wanted the book, but he had made it a rule never to buy any English book without consulting his adviser Mr. Boesen. Did I object to his doing so? Boesen, who had been selling the collection of Dr. Bandler for his estate, was an enterprising young bookseller not particularly noted for co-operation with his colleagues in the trade, but under the circumstances, having sold the book once, he could hardly advise Brunschwig not to buy it.

By the end of March, 1945, our sales from Bemis had amounted to $40,000, and what was left went into a catalogue. One description in this catalogue gave me particular satisfaction. Among the 18th-century books was a copy of one of the duodecimo editions of Goldsmith's *Deserted Village* which Bemis had bought from Rosenbach in 1926 for $475.00. These duodecimos had been characterized by T.J. Wise, Temple Scott and others as "privately printed"

Rare Books

IN

English Literature

CATALOGUE 383

The books described in this catalogue were formerly in the collection of the late Frank B. Bemis, and contain his bookplate. With few exceptions they are in uniformly fine condition.

Measurements given in the descriptions refer to the size of the leaf in inches.

Goodspeed's Book Shop, Inc.

18 Beacon Street
Boston 8, Massachusetts

and of great rarity. I devoted a page in the catalogue to exploding this myth, and, for emphasis, deflated the book by marking it $125.00. Nine years later the eminent Professor Todd published a learned dissertation on these so-called "private issues", exposing them as piracies. Discussing the tales which had given rise to the private issue fiction he remarked that though a few scholars had denied the stories "their protests have not availed against the extravagant claims of Goldsmith's bibliographers *or the raucous cries of booksellers.*"

This catalogue came out just as the Parke-Bernet auction catalogue with the English portion of Frank Hogan's library appeared. Hogan, like Bemis, had gone in heavily for English literary highspots, and inevitably a number of books turned up in both collections. How much this competition hurt us I don't know, but out of the $58,000 listed in our catalogue we sold less than 20 per cent. Today this would be considered a disaster, but I don't recall being greatly depressed by the result. Books were harder to sell thirty-five years ago. A year later Dr. W. Inglis Morse, an eccentric retired clergyman from Nova Scotia, a great benefactor of Dalhousie University and Harvard, who lived in the house that had been President Eliot's, bought the remaining 18th-century material as a Christmas present for his son-in-law, Ted Hilles, and when Louis Rabinowitz arrived with the Grolier Club's outing to Boston in 1950, and picked up what was left of the Lambs, we had few of Mr. Bemis's books to show.

In retrospect, the whole transaction seems like small potatoes. We had invested $65,000 and a great deal of hard work to get a profit of $45,000 over a period of five years. But it was a valuable episode in my education in the book trade. I wish I had the lot back today!

* * * * * * * * *

HOGAN

F.H. DAY, surviving partner in the long defunct publishing firm Copeland and Day, died in 1933, leaving the bulk of his estate to the Dedham, Massachusetts, Historical Society. Day's house in nearby Norwood, now occupied by the Norwood Historical Society, was large and rambling but its owner, though in reasonably good health, had for the last thirty years kept himself to his bedroom and was rarely seen except by the servants who attended to him.

To Julius Tuttle, librarian of the Massachusetts Historical Society, and head of the Dedham Society, fell the responsibility of disposing of Day's real and personal effects. Tuttle called on us to appraise the library and correspondence, and eventually, after what seemed to us interminable delays, to buy the collection, which proved to be a fantastic one.

The bulk of it, of course, consisted of the overstock of Copeland and Day publications. Many of these were of little value, but there were small remainders of books by Stephen Crane, Father Tabb, Louise Guiney and other American writers of the 'nineties. There was an especially fine run of Crane, including one of the three copies bound in vellum of *The Black Riders*; several copies of the same on Japan paper as well as several letters and a manuscript of the second poem in *The Black Riders*. Copeland and Day were American agents for John Lane, and consequently there were mint copies of many of Lane's publications including several of Oscar Wilde. There was a batch of proofs of illustrations and many original drawings for title-

41

THE NINETIES IN AMERICA & ENGLAND

GOODSPEED'S CATALOGUE No. 225

pages, &c., including a drawing by Beardsley of Guinevere which we adapted for use on the cover of a catalogue based on the collection.

The Wilde material included a fine letter to Day in which the writer incorporated the text of his famous sonnet on the sale of Keats's letters to Fanny Brawne. This splendid manuscript appeared in our catalogue at $250.00. At the time it attracted no buyer. A decade later, after passing through our hands, it reappeared at auction in New York, where it realized $165.00!

Day had an important collection of Keats, including letters and association books, as well as Fanny Brawne's letters to the poet. The latter, in accordance with Day's ambiguously expressed wishes, Tuttle sent to the Keats Museum at Hampstead. (There is an entertaining account of Day's Keats collection and its eventual dispersal in Rollins and Parrish's *Keats and the Bostonians*, Cambridge, 1951.) The most valuable part of the Keats collection was placed in our hands for sale, quite independent of the main library, which we had bought out-right, in January, 1935.

The Keats material thus consigned to us included the *Poems* of 1817, inscribed on the title-page to "W. Wordsworth with the Author's sincere Reverence," *Lamia*, inscribed "To Wm. Hazlitt Esq. with the Author's sincere respects," B.R. Haydon's copy of *Endymion*, a manuscript containing two sonnets, no less than three letters from Keats to Fanny Brawne, and one to Mrs. Wylie.

With Frank Bemis out of the market, we had few local buyers for material of this caliber, though Hyde Cox, then a freshman at Harvard, bought one of the letters to Fanny and the one to Mrs. Wylie only a few days after the lot came to us. These are now in the Keats collection at Harvard. Another of the letters to Fanny Brawne went to J.K. Lilly in 1937.

Frank J. Hogan had bought his first rare book a mere four years earlier, perhaps encouraged by Mrs. Edward L. Doheny whose husband Hogan had just successfully defended in the famous bribery suit which followed the Teapot Dome scandal. Buyers for five figure books were as scarce as the books themselves in the early 'thirties, so

Hogan's fame was widespread, but he had never been our customer. A letter to his Washington office describing the *Poems* only produced a wire from the William Penn Hotel asking for a quotation. He was in Pittsburgh "indefinitely" trying another famous case, that of Andrew Mellon before the Board of Tax Appeals.

We met for dinner in Pittsburgh a few days later and after dinner in his suite he went over the Keats collection. When we came to the letter to Fanny Brawne he beamed:

> These are the letters that Endymion wrote
> To one he loved in secret and apart
> And now, the travelers of the auction mart
> Bargain and bid for each poor blotted note.

With the self-satisfied air of a conjurer pulling his rabbit out of the hat, I reached into my brief-case, saying: "I just happen to have with me a manuscript of that Wilde sonnet."

When the sale was completed, Hogan said, "Now, you must get me a manuscript copy of Kit Morley's sonnet on the same subject which ends:

> The soul of Adonais, like a star
> Eight hundred dollars, Doctor R!

The sonnet was written to commemorate the sale of a letter from Keats to Fanny Brawne in the Buxton Forman sale on March 15, 1920.

I had no doubt that Morley would oblige with a manuscript copy. To my surprise, he demurred, saying that he had made but two copies, one for Rosenbach, the other for Mitchell Kennerley and that for sentimental reasons he would make no more. I consequently applied to Kennerley, who held me up for $150 for his copy, which went to Hogan at cost.

I recall that the evening was a late one, and as it drew to a close Hogan presented me with a copy of the catalogue of fiction from his library which had just been on exhibition for a gathering of the

Smith College Alumnae Association, inscribed "Blots and all — on the day we met and I fell."

Two years later in 1937, Hogan exhibited the Keats books, and the letter to Fanny Brawne together with a few other pieces at a Zamorano Club luncheon. An attractive catalogue compiled by the owner, and privately printed at the Ward Ritchie Press was issued in 1938. Hogan sent me a copy with the generous inscription — "Good friend — good bookman, who brought me the gems of this." It would appear, if the account given by Wolf and Fleming in *Rosenbach* can be relied on, that the Keats *Poems* and the letter to Fanny Brawne had made a previous visit to the Zamorano Club, on July 24, 1935:

> The demonstration of how [Rosenbach] sold books was given by Frank J. Hogan, who brought along as exhibits a number of the choicest items he had secured from the Doctor. The reaction of the Californians to these literary treasures, including a copy of Keats's *Poems* presented to Wordsworth and a letter from the young poet to Fanny Brawne, was rather naive, but charming.

Perhaps the bland assumption by Rosenbach's biographers that he was the purveyor of this treasure is evidence of an equally charming naiveté.

It was in 1938 that the famous manuscript of *Auld Lang Syne* in Burns's handwriting was placed in our hands for sale. The manuscript had a long and distinguished provenance: for years the property of William Pickering, it had on Pickering's death been sold at Sotheby's in 1855, Henry Stevens being the successful bidder. It passed from Stevens to J.V.L. Pruyn, a distinguished lawyer, industrialist, and Congressman from Albany. After Pruyn's death it passed to his daughter Mrs. Charles S. Hamlin by whom it was consigned to us. The highly sentimental strain in Hogan's make-up marked him as an obvious prospect for this sentimental ballad. I recall spending a good part of a day in Hogan's Washington office, mostly waiting between appointments. At long last, as the day drew to a close and no sale concluded, Hogan invited me to his house for dinner. My lawyer friend Horace Moulton, who was also in Washington on business for the day, was waiting for me in the Mayflower lobby. I had him paged and cancelled our meeting for dinner. Hogan's house on Massachusetts Avenue, very elegant in the Tiffany manner, was hardly the place for business talk, and not until we were on our way to the railroad station did we get down to the protracted dickering which Hogan always considered essential, and which I have always disliked (and at which I have never been very good). Before we arrived at the station we had reached an impasse. Partly to fill out the conversation, perhaps, I remarked that the friend whom I was to meet at the station was the son of the Chief Justice of Vermont. By an odd coincidence Judge Moulton and Hogan had just been together on a panel of the American Bar Association, the discovery of which circumstance left me somewhat chagrined as Hogan would, naturally, have insisted that the young lawyer join us at dinner. At any rate, Hogan came with me to the train gate where, characteristically, we struck a last minute deal and I took the parcel containing *Auld Lang Syne* out from under my arm and handed it to Hogan as I entered the gate to the train.

* * * * * * * * *

AT AUCTION

IT HAD BEEN the practice of some members of the trade to use the auction room as a means of disposing of their stock—sometimes for the purpose of liquidating slow moving merchandise, and sometimes to tap a wider market for sensational pieces. It cannot be questioned that, in the excitement of the sale room, fantastic sums are occasionally realized.

For a number of reasons, we have rarely used the auction for this purpose. The auction gallery is the bookseller's competition both in buying and selling. This is particularly true in the United States, where the auction houses have encouraged participation by the carriage trade, whereas in England the auctioneers have tended to cater to the booksellers. Furthermore, selling by auction is a great gamble, and prices fetched by one's own consignments are frequently disappointing.

On occasion, however, we have, for one reason or another, departed from custom and consigned show pieces to auction. One of these occasions took place early in 1936, when we acquired the manuscript of Longfellow's *Wreck of the Hesperus*. At the end of the manuscript was a letter from Longfellow written on January 2, 1840, offering the poem to Epes Sargent, currently associated with George Pope Morris on the *New York Mirror*, for twenty-five dollars.

The manuscript included a sixth stanza, which had been cancelled by the author, and had not appeared in print. The poem was rejected by Sargent, but was quickly snapped up by Park Benjamin for the *New World*, in which journal it appeared on January 11, 1840.

Arthur Swann, who was at this time a Vice-President of the Anderson Galleries, paid us one of his not infrequent visits, and was shown the Longfellow manuscript. He begged us to put it up at auction. W.T.H. Howe was the hottest prospect for the piece, and since he was not our customer, and known as a heavy buyer at auction, it seemed like a good idea.

Together with a juvenile manuscript of Emerson, which we had also consigned, the *Wreck of the Hesperus* appeared in the catalogue of the Marsden J. Perry sale on March 11 and 12.

When the catalogue appeared, I had a telephone call from Longfellow's grandson, the late Henry Wadsworth Longfellow Dana, who was the custodian of the Longfellow collection at Craigie House, inquiring whether we would execute a bid on his behalf, adding that he would go to $300.00. I told him that we were the consignors, that the manuscript had cost us considerably more than that, and that we were prepared to buy it up to a thousand dollars or more. With a naiveté typical of Dana, he said that he quite understood. Would I mind if he sent a bid of $300.00 to the Galleries? Of course not, I said, adding that to do so would be a waste of time.

I was sent to New York to attend the sale. The Emerson went for a hundred dollars at the evening session. The Longfellow came up the following afternoon. Walter Hill, as always, was on hand representing W.T.H. Howe. The bidding began slowly, and I had to enter it early to keep the auction alive, Hill being the only other bidder. It went so slowly, indeed, that there were but the two of us bidding. I had expected to carry the bidding up to twelve hundred dollars, but I panicked at a thousand and the lot was at the point of being knocked down to Hill when George Grasberger walked into the room. Grasberger was a bookseller who had served an apprenticeship with Rosenbach and had built something of a commission business in books and manuscripts with wealthy Philadelphians. He was a familiar figure in the sale rooms. Just as the hammer was about to fall, he entered the bidding and pushed Hill (who rarely gave up in such a contest) up to $3000 before dropping out.

It must be remembered, however, that the auction market is a very uncertain one, and great rarities sometimes go for far less than their true value because of the cataloguer's ineptitude.

One such "sleeper" to which I have referred earlier appeared in the Harmsworth sale at Sotheby's in 1949. The catalogue entry read as follows:

> Cotton, J. *Milk for Babes drawn out of the Breasts of Both Testaments*, 8ll., First edition, red levant morocco by Riviere, g.e. [Church cat., 473; not in *Sabin*], *Rare*. 8vo. 1646.

A magnificent specimen of undercataloguing by omitting to quote the subtitle: "Chiefly, for the spiritual nourishment of *Boston* Babes in either *England*: But may be of like use for any children," not only was the flavor of the book lost, but the fact that this was without doubt the first American juvenile. Nor was it pointed out that the little book was an ancestor of the New England Primer in which it was reprinted many times after 1690. Nor, indeed, did the catalogue do justice to rarity; only two other copies were (or are) known: one in the British Museum, the other (wanting two leaves) in the Huntington Library.

Greatly excited at the possibility of catching a sleeper we cabled a bid (as I recall) of £750 or thereabouts and were naturally delighted when it fell to us at a small fraction of the bid. A few months later J.K. Lilly was happy to pay us what we had bid.

* * * * * * * * *

A FLAW IN THE TITLE

A BOOK THIEF is a great nuisance. Not only does he steal your property, but unless you are alert, he can make you a fence unaware, and thus steal your good name as well. My first encounter with one of these characters was in 1927, when I was new in the business. This man came into the shop with a little run of presentation copies of books by E.A. Robinson, Amy Lowell and other poets of the time. Each was inscribed by its author to Edmund R. Brown, a gentleman with whom I was not acquainted, and indeed, of whom I had never heard. The seller assured me that he was himself Mr. Brown.

Brown was, in fact, a rather active publisher who had done business under the trade name of Four Seas Publishing Company, and was then, as later, engaged in publishing books for the account of authors who were unable to find an outlet through regular commercial publishers. He had thus introduced many writers of prominence to the world. It was under his imprint that the literary career of William Faulkner was launched. Of all this I was ignorant, and when having catalogued part of my purchase a few months later, I was confronted by the real Mr. Brown, catalogue in hand asking for the return of his books, my embarrassment was considerable.

Both of us wanted to have the thief prosecuted, if he could be found. Suspicion was directed toward one of Brown's ex-employees, and when, on some pretext or other, I made a call on the presumed culprit, I was certain that we had the right man.

The police were summoned, and our suspect was brought before Judge Adlow in the district court of Suffolk County. Brown and I

50

told our story. The accused denied having taken the books or having sold them to me. The judge refused to issue a warrant for the man's arrest, remarking to me: "It is months since you bought the books. You had never seen this man before, and your identification would never stand up under cross-examination. You might well end up on the losing end of a suit for false arrest." The judge was quite right, of course. I returned the unsold books to their owner and had the embarrassing task of retrieving the others from customers who had bought them from me.

Of course, every bookseller, however careful he may be, has suffered the embarrassment of finding that he has been made an unwitting receiver of stolen goods. One instance of this sort which occurred in the 'twenties resulted in a quarrel between my father and that Grand Panjandrum, the late A. Edward Newton.

It all began with an impression of Revere's famous Boston Massacre engraving which my father had sold to Rosenbach. The first part of the episode is recounted in C.E. Goodspeed's *Yankee Bookseller*:

> I recall an unusual experience connected with the purchase of one of Revere's *Boston Massacre* prints years ago. It was brought to me one morning by a stranger of middle age, a decorator by trade, from Hartford, Connecticut. The condition of the engraving was not of the best, and my offer did not satisfy the vendor. 'That is just what I shall have to pay for it.' 'Very well,' I replied, 'it is all that I can give for it in that state.' Two days later he returned to accept the proffered amount.
>
> About that time I had received an inquiry from Doctor Rosenbach in New York for Revere's *Boston Massacre* and I sent this one to him. A fortnight had passed when the man from whom I bought it reappeared, much agitated. He gave an account of his relation to the print as follows: An auctioneer of his acquaintance was the owner

51

of a lot of absorbent cotton and he was trying to sell it for him. Not meeting with much success he asked for money for travelling expenses. His appeal being refused with a plea of 'no funds,' the possibility of selling the *Boston Massacre* then hanging in the auctioneer's office was discussed. Finally the auctioneer told him that if he could sell it for a certain amount he might apply the money to his expense account. With this agreement he went out to make inquiries about the engraving, and after his conversation with me, returned to get it. The auctioneer was out so he took it from the wall, brought it to me, and after taking time to consider my offer, sold it as narrated above. After making this statement he said, 'Now, Mr. Goodspeed, this fellow denies the agreement, says that I took the print without authority, and has had me arrested for larceny!' 'When does the case come up?' I asked. He replied that he was summoned to be in court that morning.

Of course there was nothing for me to do but to go up to the Courthouse and see the thing through. It was just a clearcut case of two parties denying *in toto* the statements made by the other. One was lying. Which one was it? I think the judge was puzzled, and his decision bears out that thought, for although he found my man guilty, he put him on probation.

This left me in the embarrassing position of having purchased, sold, and delivered a print in which I had no title. I therefore wrote to Doctor Rosenbach explaining the matter. Fortunately he was able to help me out of the dilemma by returning it. I then telephoned the legal owner to call for the print, but he failed to do so. After various reminders he called me six months later and said, 'Why don't you buy that print of me? You'll never get anything out of the man from whom you got it; perhaps you can sell it and get your money back that way.' He was wrong in thinking that I would not get my money refunded, as I had already been reimbursed three-quarters of the amount. I got the balance later. However, I said, 'I will give you what I paid for it before.' He accepted the offer and the engraving then became my property.

It subsequently developed that Rosenbach had sold the print to Newton, who wanted it to use as a frontispiece to his second collection of papers, *A Magnificent Farce*. Newton returned the print to Rosenbach when the title proved faulty. We were, of course, unaware that he had bought the engraving from Rosenbach.

Newton, in the course of a visit to Boston in 1926, mentioned his interest in a Massacre print, not, however, revealing that he had been Rosenbach's customer for the one that passed through our hands before. It so happened that a Mr. Cutler of Boston owned a copy then on loan to the Museum of Fine Arts in Boston, for the purchase of which we had been negotiating, though fruitlessly. At my father's suggestion Newton went to the Museum to see the print, which he assumed (incorrectly) to be the identical one of which he had had temporary possession.

In March, 1927, we issued a catalogue of the Sumner Hollingsworth collection of Americana. In it was illustrated an impression of the rare reengraving of the Massacre print by Jonathan Mulliken the Newburyport clockmaker. From a glance at the illustration, Newton evidently assumed it to be the Revere print and shot off a wire ordering it, together with four other items. When the engraving was reported sold he was furious and dispatched a long and abusive letter, concluding: "Had anyone told me that you would have treated me with such discourtesy, I should have said 'no respectable bookseller would be guilty of such a trick' — and I should have been mistaken."

A long letter recounting the facts failed to mollify the irate Philadelphian whose secretary wrote on the 8th: "Mr. Newton directs me to return the items you recently sent him and instructs me to ask you to remove his name from your mailing list."

There was a curious sequel to the Newton affair. A few years later, in 1930, to be exact, we sold to Chauncey Tinker a copy of *A Week on the Concord and Merrimack Rivers* inscribed by Thoreau to his abolitionist friend, Parker Pillsbury. It was not exactly in Tink's field of collecting, but he did buy an American book on occasion. Much to our surprise the *Week* surfaced again in the Newton sale in 1941 with a letter from Tinker to Newton about the book. The book and the letter were bought at Newton's sale by Michael Papantonio for the late W. Luther Lewis, whose collection is now in Texas Christian University. Repeated requests to that institution for a copy of that letter have to date been denied. I confess to a continuing curiosity as to its contents.*

No doubt because of this unfortunate episode, Newton inserted a gratuitous slur on "Goodspeed's of Boston" in *This Book-Collecting Game* a year later. A sentence in the same book linking Quaritch of

---

* A copy of the letter has since been supplied to me, and I append it.

The Commander Hotel
Cambridge, Massachusetts

At the Elm

Apr. 14. 1930.

Dear Ned:

A Week on the Concord goes to you to-day from Dunster House bookshop. The price, as you will see, is $1500, but I got it for $1400, for you. So send me your check. If you won't have it, I'll be glad to get it. I used to know Parker Pillsbury in Concord N.H., where my aunt lived. The priceless condition of the book is due to the fact that he kept all his books wrapped up in brown paper.

I got *Two Years before the Mast* for $112.50, but it is not in such good state as yours.

It is a bum experience to come back & get to work—but three weeks more brings me to the end.

I had a grand time in Daylesford.

Yours always therefore,

Tink

London with the knock-out resulted in a threatened law suit and the cancellation of the offending leaf in the English edition.

A less unhappy incident arising out of a questioned title occurred in 1942. It had to do with a copy of the broadside Declaration of Independence printed at Salem in July, 1776. This "official" printing of the great document was made at the direction of the Council of the Massachusetts Colony, which decreed that

> a copy [be] sent to the Ministers of each parish . . . and that they severally be required to read the same to their respective Congregations, as soon as Divine Service is ended, in the afternoon, on the first Lord's Day they shall have received it . . . and after such publication thereof, to deliver the said Declaration to the Clerks of their several Towns, or Districts; also are hereby required to record the same in their respective Town or District Book, there to remain as a perpetual Memorial thereof.

In early December a lady brought in to us a collection of revolutionary broadsides which had come down in the family from her ancestor Timothy Alden (1771-1839) clergyman, antiquarian and compiler of *A Collection of American Epitaphs*. Alden's maternal grandfather was the Reverend Habijah Weld, minister in Attleboro. Among the broadsides was a copy of the Salem Declaration addressed "For the Revd. Mr. Weld, Attleborough."

The Declaration broadside was sold to Matt B. Jones, then President of the New England Telephone and Telegraph Company, and the leading collector of Americana in the Boston area. Jones immediately presented the piece to the American Antiquarian Society, in whose collection it remained until after his death in 1940. In 1942, the Society, with whom it had proved to be a duplicate, sold it back to us, and it was featured in *The Month at Goodspeed's* for June.

Prodded, I suppose, by some local antiquarians the Solicitor for the City of Attleboro had come to us making a claim for the broadside, on the grounds that under the terms of its issuance, it properly belonged to the City. Being a legal matter I sent the lawyer down to the office of our attorney Horace Moulton, then in private practice on State Street.

Because of the manner in which it was distributed, this is a *relatively* common edition of the Declaration (Michael Walsh in his check-list locates eleven others) and since it comes on the market occasionally, it seemed important to establish once and for all what the legal status of copies sent to the ministers of other towns might be. Accordingly, we agreed with the City of Attleboro to have the matter tried in court, the understanding being that whichever side lost in the Superior Court would take the case up on appeal to the Supreme Judicial Court for adjudication.

The case was accordingly heard by Judge Goldberg of the Superior Court who, after the lapse of a considerable time (a year or more I believe), found for us. There were a number of issues involved, so we anticipated the outcome on appeal with interest. We never knew, of course, on what ground Judge Goldberg's finding had been made. To our disappointment the City was not inclined to spend the money that would be entailed in appealing, so we still do not know the answer to the crucial question: Do the words "to record the same in their respective Town or District Book, there to remain as a perpetual Memorial" refer to the text of the document or to the printed broadside as a physical entity?

Sometimes, of course, circumstantial evidence is not to be trusted. I recall an experience with one of the colorful figures in the New England book world three decades ago. He was a persistent and accomplished thief. He was a lanky backcountry farm type and suffered from tuberculosis. For several years he haunted the bookshops, where his reputation for larceny was well-known. I cannot remember that he was ever caught red-handed, but he continually turned up with stolen merchandise which he offered for sale. On more than one occasion we implored him to stay out of the shop, which he usually did for a few weeks at a time, but he always returned, swearing that he had reformed, and begging permission to browse through the shelves. This necessitated assigning a salesman to stand at his elbow, and was somewhat of a nuisance.

He appeared at Beacon Street late on one Spring afternoon with a quarto volume of eighteenth century pamphlet poems for which he asked twenty-five dollars. I asked him where he had got it. A dozen quarto poems were clearly under-priced at a couple of dollars apiece, and I was, of course, suspicious. I was assured by the seller that he had bought them from a thoroughly reputable bookseller in the neighborhood. I told him to leave the collection overnight while I could check his story. Somewhat to my surprise, I found it to be true and when our friend returned, we paid him the price he had asked. (This individual subsequently was employed by the Massachusetts State Archives and enjoyed the privilege of a stack permit in the Harvard library. Needless to say, both institutions were gold mines for him.)

A copy of the second edition of Gray's *Elegy* alone was worth the price of admission, but the great prize between the old calf covers was a copy of Samuel Johnson's very rare *Prologue . . . Spoken at the Opening of the Theatre in Drury Lane*, 1747.

Rosenbach in 1902 had acquired a copy (which he then believed to be unique) of this Johnsonian rarity, and published an elaborate facsimile edition of it with bibliographical notes by himself and a preface by Austin Dobson. I went to the Athenaeum a few doors down the street to see the facsimile. To my disappointment, that institution turned up not only the facsimile but a copy of the original which somewhat defeated my ideas of its value. When Harvard also came up with a copy I was properly discouraged. So much so, indeed, that when Chauncey Tinker came in a few days later he bought the *Prologue* at the bargain price of $500.00.

Lest the enormous mark-up on this transaction raise eyebrows, it should be noted that the piece, though offered by an operator with a bad reputation, had come from an honest (though perhaps ignorant) dealer; that each had made a profit on his cost and each had set his own price.

One can recall other instances in which books turning up under suspicious circumstances have proved to be entirely honest. I particularly recall a copy of the first American edition of the Greek New Testament, printed by Isaiah Thomas at Worcester in 1800, which was offered to us by a bookseller in 1933. It was the copy given to Ralph Waldo Emerson by his uncle Daniel R. Ripley when Emerson was a freshman at Harvard and contained the youthful Emerson's autograph in a dozen places. It contained also the blind stamp of the public library in Springfield, Massachusetts. The asking price was seven dollars and a half. The absurdly low price, coupled with the library stamp clearly suggested that the book had been stolen. I bought the book and wrote to the library from which it had come. The answer was:

> Our records state that on April 9, 1932, we sold three books as follows for cash $2.00:
> Greek Testament. Presented to
> Ralph Waldo Emerson.
> Trumbull's Sermon, 1783.
> Third Reader — Greensboro
> It is possible of course that the Greek Testament slipped by without [the 'Dup. Sold'] stamp. It was, however, legitimately sold by us.

Over the centuries books have been removed from old monastic and royal libraries under obscure circumstances. Many, of course, were sold or exchanged, and many were stolen. They have circulated for generations, passing from one owner to another, so that in time their title has become clear by reason of antiquity. This is especially true of early printed books with early monastic inscriptions.

An example of this kind of provenance is a copy of *Pietas et Gratulatio Collegii Cantabrigiensis apud Novanglos* now in my own library. A collection of poetical tributes in English, Latin and Greek to the memory of George II and to the virtues of George III, it was Harvard's emulation of similar effusions being offered by the English universities. A handsome quarto, one of the most ambitious products of the provincial press up to its time, it was printed by Green and Russell at Cambridge in 1761. As Evans remarks, it is typographically "the handsomest specimen of the printer's art produced in the American Colonies." It contains the first extensive use of Greek type in this country. The type was the property of the college library, the gift of Thomas Hollis, and was loaned by the college to the printer for use in this book. It was later destroyed in the fire which leveled Harvard Hall in 1764.

Copies of the book were printed on thick paper for presentation to the royal family and sent to Hollis in London where they might be suitably bound. My copy, which is one of these, is bound in red morocco, tooled in gilt. It was formerly in the collection of A.J. Odell, sold in 1878. In that sale catalogue it is described as the presentation copy to George III, a claim disputed by Evans who noted that George III's copy is with the rest of his library, in the British Museum. The catalogue description notes that a coat of arms had been cut out of each cover, and replaced with an ornamental patch, roughly circular in shape.

Some years back I showed this copy to Howard Nixon at the British Museum. The binding proved to be the work of Richard Montagu whom Hollis employed occasionally for special work. Still present under the patches were the arms of George III. I had the front patch removed, exposing the arms on the upper cover. It has not been unusual for members of the royal family to give away or to sell gifts for which they have no use, and evidently this book was disposed of in some such way.

The only defense a bookseller has against thieving is constant vigilance, whether it be in keeping a close watch on strange customers lest they make off with his stock, or in buying, to question as closely as possible the history of the occasional book brought in for sale. Either way there is the risk of offending perfectly innocent people, and still, after all reasonable precautions are taken, the grave danger of being victimized remains.

* * * * * * * * *

RARISSIMI

THOMAS R. ADAMS, the librarian of the John Carter Brown Library has recently compiled a catalogue of "one hundred and one books NOT in the J.C.B." His list includes fourteen pieces of which "no copy can currently be located."

One of these is a broadside printing of "the Capitall Laws of New England, as they stand now in force in the Commonwealth." This broadside is known to have been printed at Cambridge in 1642, but seems to have disappeared entirely. It is the first printed collection of American laws enacted by a legislature, and surely the cornerstone of any collection of American legal history.

Not surprisingly, a reprint of this document, listing the offenses for which death was the penalty, was reprinted (in the following year) in London. The printer was Benjamin Allen, who printed much of the early theological and political material relating to New England.

The list of offenses punishable by death, fifteen in number, includes six involving sex crimes, homicide in various forms (three), a variety of others beginning with the worship of "any other god but the Lord God," the practice of witchcraft, blasphemy, kidnapping, bearing false witness with intent "to take away any man's life," and treason.

But two copies of this London printing are known. One is in the Thomason Collection in the British Museum. The other lay formerly in the library of the Dean and Chapter of Lincoln Cathedral.

Shortly after the close of the Second World War, Bishop Dunlop, then Dean of Lincoln, was greatly concerned for the condition of the fabric of the Cathedral, and in conversation with a visitor from Boston, wondered whether this rare piece of Americana might be sold to advantage, and the proceeds used to defray the cost of needed repairs. When the Bostonian returned home, she came to us, and in 1952 Mike Walsh, in England on a holiday, called the Dean to suggest a price.

As the result of negotiations which continued over many months, it was agreed that we might offer the Laws to some public collection in Massachusetts at twelve thousand dollars (we to keep two thousand as our commission). It was 1955 before things came to this point. The logical repository of the broadside was the Massachusetts State Library, where it might be displayed beside the original manuscript of Bradford's *History of Plimouth Plantation*.

The money for such a purchase would have to come by legislative appropriation, never easily obtained for such a purpose. At the suggestion of Justice Wilkins of the Supreme Judicial Court, I applied to the Governor's Counsel Paul Reardon for an appointment with Governor Herter whom, we felt, would be sympathetic. Reardon accordingly took Mike and myself into the Governor's office the next day when he brought in the day's sheaf of bills for the executive signature. Herter heard our story, agreed that the Laws ought to be bought for the Commonwealth, and promised to include the appropriation in his supplementary budget, then in preparation for submission to the Committee on Ways and Means.

Walsh and Reardon appeared before the Committee at the budget hearing, Reardon bringing the Governor's endorsement of the appropriation and Walsh commenting that legislatures were sometimes criticized for spending money, but that in this instance they might in the end be criticized for not doing so. The legislature then, and the Committee of course, were both under Republican control. A friend of Walsh's, Michael Paul Feeney, was a member of the Committee, and remarked before the hearing that if one Republican member would go along with the Governor, the appropriation would pass. It failed to do so, and the Commonwealth lost the prize.

Bill Jackson of the Houghton had already indicated that, if it came to that, Harvard would find the money for the Law School Library. And that is what happened, a generous publishing house being the angel.

At this point the question arose as to how the broadside might safely be sent across the Atlantic. We thought that registered air mail would be the safest means. Ironically the letter in which we made the suggestion was destroyed in a disastrous plane crash at Prestwick. However, the piece of paper did arrive safely, at last, and may be seen today in the great library of the Harvard Law School.

The word *unique* as applied to a printed book has a fascination for all bibliophiles including, especially, booksellers. It is a word that crops up continually in catalogues, as "a unique copy, with presentation inscription by the author to his wife" (or son or whatever). The word here is used properly, for any book with a presentation inscription is unique as far as the inscription is concerned, just as any manuscript is so by definition.

The number of books to which the adjective may be applied in the absolute sense is not large; and such are of infrequent occurrence on the market. A good example in modern literature is Robert Frost's first printed book *Twilight* of which the poet had two copies printed. We have his word that he destroyed one of the two. The remaining copy he sold in 1940 to Earle J. Bernheimer. It appeared in the auction rooms in 1950, when it realized $3500, a price which seemed to me at the time very modest, indeed. That it went so cheaply was due, as Mr. Barrett writes, "to an egregious blunder." I let *Twilight* get away. I thought it should have been worth four or five times that amount, and before the sale I tried vainly to convince two of my collector friends that they should bid on it accordingly. Failing to convince them, I lacked the courage to back up my conviction and pursue the prize for stock. Time proved that I was right when, after another decade, it finally passed into the great Barrett collection, it did so at a figure not far from my original estimate.

In any event, *unique* is a word to be used sparingly; and the conservative cataloguer is likely to qualify it as "unrecorded and presumably unique."

In this category is the original American printing by Benjamin Franklin of Richardson's *Pamela*. Charles Evans, in the second volume of his *American Bibliography* listed three separate printings in 1744, one in Boston, one in New York and one in Philadelphia, the latter printed by Franklin. No copy of any of these printings had ever been found. It was Evans's practice, on occasion, to list books as possibly printed in this country because he had found them listed in advertisements or catalogues of American booksellers. It has often developed that no such American printings ever existed: the bookseller was merely offering imports of English books from his stock. Such are referred to by bibliographers as "ghosts," *i.e.*, books described by bibliographers, but which are indeed nonexistent.

This American *Pamela* had for years been held as one of Evans's phantoms, as indeed it was, since, insofar as we still know, there was no edition in 1744. It developed, however, that Benjamin Franklin had indeed printed an edition of the book, a copy of which had reposed for years in the library of Simmons College in Boston. It had been found and recorded in manuscript by the W.P.A. imprints survey conducted during the years of the great Depression. It was dated 1742 (1743 on the title-page of Volume II) but the printing was not completed until late in the summer of 1744.

Neither we nor, so far as I am aware, anyone outside of Simmons knew of the existence of this copy until 1968 when Dr. Park, then President of the College, called me on the phone to inquire whether there might be a market for it and at what price. It was hard to understand how the entire edition of such a substantial book (394 pages) could, with the exception of this one copy, have disappeared entirely. C. William Miller's researches, since published (*Benjamin Franklin's Philadelphia Printing*) may give the answer. That 36 sets were still on hand when Franklin sold his stock in 1748, suggests that the publication was not a commercial success and that many copies may have been scrapped.

There was obviously no problem in disposing of such a book — the earliest work of fiction printed in the American colonies, by a printer who was later to become one of the great founders of the republic. As often happens in such instances, the difficulty was in dealing with a board of trustees all of whom became, of course, instant authorities on a subject of which they had the day before known little or nothing. The method of sale, the profit to be allowed the entrepreneur, and the identity of the ultimate purchaser were all of concern to each and every individual on the board. We felt fortunate, indeed, to be permitted to handle the transaction, even though under the circumstances the profit involved was nominal, and though we had to get the seller's approval of our customer as an appropriate repository. We chose the American Antiquarian Society on whose shelves the book rests happily today. It is properly dignified by inclusion in that great institution's brochure *A Society's Chief Joys*.

Carroll Wilson had from us two books (pamphlets actually) which can properly be described as "presumably unique" and curiously enough they are both by Longfellow, printed in the last years of his life. One of them, a poem appropriately entitled "Morituri Salutamus" was written in 1875 for the occasion of the fiftieth anniversary of the graduation of his class at Bowdoin College. We found it in the library of George William Curtis at Ashfield, Massachusetts in 1935. Although the Chamberlain-Livingston bibliography notes that Longfellow had had printed a pamphlet edition of the poem, no copy of such had ever appeared. Wilson, in the catalogue of his library, argues convincingly that this copy must have been the sole surviving example. Longfellow had sent it to Curtis, who as editor of *Harper's Monthly* was to print it, with Longfellow's ms. corrections and additions. There is no copy at Craigie House or any of the other repositories in which it might be expected to be found, or as Wilson wrote: "It is one of the romances of book-collecting that so important a Longfellow first, definitely determined to be non-existent by the greatest authorities on the subject, should turn up after 70 years, and in precisely the place where it ought to have been."

The other Longfellow pamphlet, Part II of the posthumously printed *Michael Angeloe*, came to us from an obscure source (as I recall it came from a book scout), and is as Wilson remarked the only one of the great Longfellow printed first edition rarities of which only a single copy is known, "except my *Morituri Salutamus*."

I remarked at the beginning of this chapter that any inscribed copy of a book is, by definition, unique as far as the inscription is concerned. And in the same way all autograph letters are unique as well. Perhaps it may be permitted therefore, to close this section with a mention of what is to me the finest letter to have passed through our hands in my time. It was written by Benjamin Franklin in Passy to his friend Josiah Quincy on the eleventh of September 1783, days after the peace which brought the American Revolution to a close. It belonged to a Harvard classmate of mine, a descendant of the original recipient. This great letter written at such a time, when controversy with his colleagues, Adams and Jay, had been a source of trial to him concludes:

> As to the two charges of age and weakness, I must confess the first, but I am not so clear in the latter; and perhaps my adversaries may find they presumed a little too much upon it, when they ventured to attack me. But enough of these petty personalities. I quit them to rejoice with you in the peace God has blessed us with, and in the prosperity it gives us a prospect of. The definitive Treaty was signed the 3d. instant. We are now friends with England and with all mankind. May we never see another war, for in my opinion *there never was* a good war nor a bad peace . . . .
>
> B. Franklin

* * * * * * *

Perhaps such unrecorded trifles as the first publication of Thomas A. Janvier (*Woman's Daring*, Annisquam, Massachusetts (?) 1872) which appeared in our Catalogue 566 and an otherwise unknown fishing tale *Nixon's Creek* (probably by W.P. Hawes) listed in Catalogue 500 are both too inconsequential to be mentioned in the same chapter as *Pamela*, but I cannot forbear repeating here the romantic discovery of the only known copy in the original covers of a penny dreadful by J.T. Trowbridge, his first book, entitled *Kate the Accomplice, or the Preacher and the Burglar* which Paul Seybolt, authority on "First Books" found forty years ago in Essex County. Let him tell the story:

> It has occurred to me that it might be interesting to have a note here describing the circumstances surrounding my so fortunate acquisition of this possibly rarest of all American works of fiction.
>
> Now, I am not too sure of the date, since it is a long time ago, now, but my best recollection is that it was in May or June of 1935. Frank Willson and I had journeyed down to Danvers in my old red Ford coupe (with the rumble seat) and stopped to call on Back Number Wilkins. Our reason for this was that Frank had learned that Back Number had recently found a lot of odd numbers of some obscure West Coast periodical that Webfoot thought might contain some Mark Twain material. I do not recall the name of it. I do recall that Frank drew blank, since aside from Stoddard and a few other minor California contributors, the thing was nothing. No Twain anyway.
>
> It was a bright sunshiny day, a Saturday, and whilst waiting for Frank to unearth some priceless and unknown MT material I was wandering around out in the yard in front of the old barn. I noticed that Back Number's truck was pulled up alongside it and that there was a small mound of magazines in the body of the old heap. I went

KATE,

THE ACCOMPLICE,

OR THE

PREACHER AND BURGLAR.

ACTON IN SEARCH OF THE BURGLARS.

BY PAUL CREYTON.

BOSTON:
JONES'S PUBLISHING HOUSE, 82 WASHINGTON STREET.
H. LONG & BROTHER, 32 ANN STREET, NEW YORK.
1849.

over and casually pawed it over. It was a long run of the *Atlantic Monthly*, broken, but quite respectable. He had trucked it in from Newburyport that morning.

The year continuity seemed to be from around 1855 to somewhere in the eighties, and noting several numbers containing installments of Henry James' *Portrait of a Lady*, I decided to see if I couldn't get the complete novel in the parts. Incidentally, I did, and I also found every number of Hardy's *Trumpet Major*. Not a bad feat, even in those days.

Well, being quite pleased with myself, and figuring that Back Number wouldn't charge me more than a dime a copy (those were dull days, if you remember), I dug down into the bottom of the pile to see if I could find some *Autocrat* parts, knowing that Carroll Wilson lacked several numbers with the wrappers intact. As I was pawing around, pulling and hauling at the various numbers (and they were all in dandy shape) this piece, somewhat thinner than the others and with no lettering on the backstrip turned up.

I included it with my Hardys and Jameses and Brother Wilkins, bless him, nicked me a dime apiece. It was the best three bucks I ever spent in my life.

Dante's *Divine Comedy* was very popular with printers of the fifteenth century, and many illustrated editions of this then modern classic appeared from 1481 on. The edition most famous and most sought after is the first one printed by Nicolaus Lavrentii at Florence in 1481. A handsome folio, it contains illustrations engraved on copper by Baldini. The intention was to supply one plate for each canto (a hundred in all), but in fact only nineteen appear to have been engraved. The printer, in laying out the volume, left a blank space before each canto, in which the illustration was to be placed; the original plan was to print the copper plate illustrations directly on the blank spaces provided, and in all copies the first two were so printed.

In some copies the third was also printed in the text, the remainder being separately printed and pasted in the appropriate spaces. Evidently neither method was wholly practical for in many copies only the first two (or three) appear.

A copy of this famous book was stored (with other books) in a Providence bank vault when the disastrous flood of 1938 inundated the downtown section. The books were, of course, badly water-stained, but not, it appeared, irreparably. They were sold to us, as I recall, by the bank or insurance company which had taken them over as salvage. The Dante was in two ways a remarkable copy. It contained three elaborately illuminated initials in gold and many colors. Although only two of the three engravings were present, this was one of the tallest copies known, a very important feature, since the first illustration appears at the bottom of the first leaf of text, and in copies that are trimmed at all the illustration is shaved at the foot. The book was sent to London for restoration, and when it came back from the binder it was a splendid copy indeed. We featured it in the issue of *The Month* for October, 1939. (This issue by the by started out with one of Dodge's finest editorials.)

> . . . the news from Europe makes it difficult for [the editor] to keep his faith in the eternal values of the rare and primary things that Goodspeed's sells. This funk is only a passing mood, however, and once beyond the fascination of the first flaming headlines and after the war has settled down to what looks to be a long spell of dogged insanity, he will shake off the dishonorable apprehension that old books, old prints, and old manuscripts are trivial things in a world where bombs are falling . . .

In charge of rare books at the Boston Public Library at the time was a brilliant scholar from Hungary who was having considerable success in popularizing the Library's collections through his writing, particularly in a sort of bibliographical house organ *More Books*, a publication that enjoyed a wide and well-deserved following. He was not generally popular with the local book trade, having a predeliction for the more scholarly and fashionable booksellers of Europe. He had a partiality for fifteenth century editions of Dante, and when the reproduction in *The Month* caught his eye, he called me in great excitement. He asked me about the condition of the copy (fully spelt out in our description); I said it was a fine one though it had been washed. I sent it up by messenger, who returned shortly thereafter with the package unopened, as he refused to look at a copy that had been washed.

There were no other orders in spite of the price (which I decline to repeat here — the curious may find it in *The Month at Goodspeed's*, XI, 1, 8). Disheartened, I later subwayed out to Cambridge and showed the book to Philip Hofer, who was delighted with it, beat me down twenty per cent and gave me his check. "Now," I said, "you should know that the B.P.L. turned it down because it is washed." "Tell them," said Hofer, "that I now have three copies of the book, and that this is the best."

Two or three years later, my friend from the B.P.L. came by my desk on his way to the Americana department. I showed him a late fifteenth century Dante which he had waved aside. "I am spoiled," he said. "I have just bought a magnificent copy of the 1481 Dante from Mr. Hofer." "I wonder," I remarked, "whether it could be the copy you turned down when I showed it to you a few years back?"

"No, indeed," he replied. "This copy has a beautifully illuminated first page." Fishing in my desk for the copy of *The Month*, I showed him the reproduction, asking whether this were indeed the copy in question. He read through the description. When he came to the price, he said "and you sold it to Hofer for that amount?" "No," said I. "He beat me down a hundred dollars." "What did you pay him?" I never got an answer.

Although the opportunites of buying collections of incunabula in the Boston area are few, I have always been partial to specimens of early printing. A small but choice collection from an old New England estate administered by John Bianchi came to us in the late 'thirties. It was perhaps because of this that the late Howard Goodhart took to dropping in on us when in town. As I look over our ledgers, it is evident that we were not significant contributors to his great collection of Mediaeval texts (now mostly at Bryn Mawr) but he was very friendly, and I learned a good bit about early books from him. Lathrop Harper in those days was the leading dealer in the field in this country. He was always friendly and generous with young booksellers. I can remember particularly the magnificent copy of Breydenbach's *Peregrinatio in terram sanctam*, the great illustrated travel book printed by Erhard Reuwich at Mainz in 1486 which came from Harper's. It had been bought by Douglas Parsonage during one of Harper's absences in Europe. The old man was not wholly immune to jealousy, and I think it disturbed him that so fine a book could be bought by a subordinate. I recall that a few weeks later Harper mentioned the transaction to my father, and hoped that I hadn't been stuck.

In 1968 the Council of the Grolier Club, feeling both a spatial and financial pinch, determined to put on the market a considerable portion of the collection of early printed books which had been given to the Club by David Wolfe Bruce, and exhibited at the Club in 1894. A small pamphlet catalogue of the exhibition was followed a year later by an elaborately illustrated folio *Description of the Early Printed Books Owned by the Grolier Club*, in which the collection was described more thoroughly. The collection was an important one, having been assembled by two practicing printers to illustrate the history of the art in its early years.

The Council offered forty-six of the Bruce Incunables to a number of booksellers who were members of the Club, to be sold *en bloc* to the highest bidder. When the bids were opened, the librarian, Gabriel Austin, telephoned me to announce that ours was the highest bid. The collection was a great prize. The earliest book in it was St. Thomas Aquinas's *Super quarto libro Sententiarum* from the press of Peter Schoeffer in 1469. Though lacking the first leaf, it was otherwise complete, with the final leaf, with the colophon and

Schoeffer's printer's mark. A reproduction of this leaf was used as the frontispiece of the 1895 *Description*.

The rarest, most important, was the *Chronica summorum pontificum imperatorumque* of Riccobaldus Ferrariensis, printed by Joannes Philippus de Lignamine at Rome in 1474. Lignamine, a native of Messina, was the first native Italian printer. His books were printed, for the most part, in small editions of 125 to 150 copies "suggesting" according to J.V. Scholderer, "that he looked for his profits rather to rewards from patrons than to ordinary sales."

The *Chronica* in particular is a legendary rarity; Dibdin, in the early nineteenth century, believed that there were but two copies in England, and in addition to the Grolier copy, only two (one in the Morgan Library, and one imperfect in the Annmary Brown Memorial in Providence) are recorded in America.

The significance of this very rare book in the history of printing lies in the reference to Gutenberg (as having printed 300 sheets a day) and to Sweynheym and Pannartz's introduction of printing into Italy in 1464.

Brunet describing the volume as "tres rare," noted "Il y a des exemplaires qui diffèrent des autres dans les derniers feuillets," referring to the fact that in some copies the compositor omitted several lines of text in the final leaf. The copies in the British Museum, J.P. Morgan and Annmary Brown collections are of this variety. When the error was discovered, the leaf was reset to include the missing lines. As a result the text on the last page was lengthened and the word "Finis" was crowded out, suggesting that the final leaf was wanting. Indeed, the Grolier Club's published catalogue described the book as defective. While I had been working on my estimate of the books for preparing our bid, it became necessary to compare the two variants, to establish the collation. To this end I stopped in at the Morgan Library and asked to see its copy. By a curious coincidence, sitting at the desk was a member of the Council of the Grolier Club which had authorized the sale of the collection. As he brought the *Chronica* out for my inspection he enquired whether I had a copy. My answer was in the negative (I had not yet bought the lot) and he made the astonishing remark that the Grolier Club would love to own one!

My first estimate on the collection had been in the area of $15,000, but as I wanted to be sure of being in the running, at least, had added $3,000 in "insurance" which, as it developed, was about the spread between us and the next bidder. Within a fortnight, the under-bidders were on the doorstep looking for books that I might have underpriced.

The bidders for the collection had included most of the American specialists in early printing, but for some reason Hans Kraus had chosen not to compete. Months afterward my friend Jack Kebabian of Kraus's staff came in on a visit to Boston and asked to look over what was left of the collection. Among the remains was a very fine copy of the *Etymologiae* of Isidorus Hispalensis printed at Augsburg by Günther Zainer in 1472. This treatise contains what is generally described as the first printed map. A reproduction of this map, in gilt, adorns the front cover of Kraus's catalogue *Monumenta Cartographica* which appeared a year or so later.

One of the many glories of fifteenth century book-making is the beautiful two-volume edition of Homer printed at Florence in 1488 by Bartolommeo di Libri from type designed by Demetrios Damilas. This is the first edition of Homer's works in Greek, and the first printed *Odyssey* in any language. An odd volume (Volume II, containing the *Odyssey*) was sold by the London Library at Sotheby's in 1966. It was bought by Maggs who later sold it to Bill Fletcher who needed it for the sake of one leaf which he needed to make up a set.

Fletcher, whose unassuming shop in Cecil Court belies the rich stock to be found below stairs, not to say the acuity of its proprietor, has many friends in and out of the trade.

I spent a week in London in February 1968 and stopped at Fletcher's shop on Saturday afternoon to say good-bye. I pulled the crippled odd volume of Homer from the shelf and remarked that it looked like a "breaker" — the bookseller's term for a book that is to be sold by the leaf (or, in the case of illustrated books, for the plates as separate prints). This is, generally speaking, a highly reprehensible practice unless the book is (as in this case) seriously defective. We have since sold most of the volume a page at a time.

Two or three months later a wealthy Bostonian and Trustee of a St. Grottlesex school asked us to help him find a suitable retirement gift for a professor of Greek at the school. I recommended the 1488 Homer as being appropriate for the purpose. I thought a copy might be found for two or three thousand dollars, since it is not a particularly rare book.

It developed, however, that the only copy on the market was the very fine Shuckburgh copy which was then held by a New York bookseller at what I considered an immodest figure. Surprisingly, our customer didn't flinch, and the retiring schoolmaster was the recipient of what must be one of the handsomest retirement gifts of all time.

* * * * * * *

Rosalie V. Halsey's *Forgotten Books of the American Nursery, a History of the Development of the American Story-Book* was published in 1911. It was the first general book on the subject, and it bore the imprint of Charles E. Goodspeed, an antiquarian bookseller. Only seven hundred copies were printed. The published price was six dollars a copy and four hundred were sold in the first ten years after publication. Not until 1947, thirty-six years after publication, did the small original edition go out of print. By 1970, a copy realized forty-five dollars at auction, and reprints today are offered by two different publishers, one of them at nearly six times the published price of the original.

That Miss Halsey's pioneer treatise bore the imprint of an antiquarian bookseller rather than that of a publishing house is not particularly remarkable, for dealers in old and rare books from the time of Rosenbach's Uncle Moses Polock on down have delighted in the charm of these relics of children long since departed.

And booksellers, into whose hands these little books have fallen, often as unconsidered trifles, have cherished them and made collections, many of which have found their way on to the shelves of institutions while others, dispersed, continue to give pleasure to bibliophiles.

Thus, the original publisher of Miss Halsey's book offered his own collection in 1936. The first substantial catalogue had been issued by Gumuchian & Company of Paris in 1930. It was a handsome quarto of two volumes, bound, in the French manner in paper wrappers, and sold for twenty-five dollars — a large price in those days, though it has recently sold for as much as three hundred and fifty dollars, while a one-volume reprint may be had for forty. The catalogue of the collection of A.S.W. Rosenbach published in 1933, though not a sale catalogue, was still the catalogue of a bookseller's books. It remains an important work of reference, second only to d'Alté Welch's recently published and less pretentious, though more exhaustive, *Bibliography of American Children's Books*.

It was Rosenbach who, from his Uncle Moses Polock, had inherited remainders of children's books published by Jacob Johnson, the eighteenth century Philadelphia bookseller-publisher, portions of which are still owned by Rosenbach's successor, John Fleming. Thus these juveniles have remained "in print," as it were, through successive owners for nearly two centuries. A record, surely, at least in this country.

Walter Schatzki and the late Benjamin Tighe have built successive collections for sale *en bloc*. The Schatzki collection is now in the New York Public Library. Several of Tighe's collections were sold to the American Antiquarian Society, and another, of non-American books, went to the University of California at Los Angeles.

The private collections of the late d'Alté Welch, Edgar S. Oppenheimer and Col. David McKell are too well known to require more than a mention here, but three Boston collectors have been less celebrated.

Edward Percival Merritt, a Boston banker, had a fine collection of Newbery imprints (his Horace Walpole collection, now at Harvard is better known) which were sold to Goodspeed's Book Shop after his death. He commissioned D.B. Updike to design a little typographic book-plate for use in his juveniles, and books containing it occasionally turn up in the antiquarian trade. He was the author of several privately printed books, one of which, entitled *The History of Little Billy & His Grand-Pa. A Tale for Young and Old Adorn'd with Cuts,* was printed by D.B. Updike at the Merrymount Press. The first edition, consisting of two copies was followed by a second of eleven copies. "Grand-Pa" in the tale was Merritt's friend George Lyman Kittredge, who is pictured with a cocktail shaker, referred to in the story as "Grand-Pa's rattle." This cut was engraved for this purpose by W.A. Dwiggins. Both in style and typography the little book is modelled on Newbery's eighteenth century toy-books.

Another and less selective buyer of juveniles was Beatrice Gunn, who had worked on the old *Youth's Companion.* A frowzy but pleasant little spinster, she haunted the second-hand shops and accumulated an immense collection which she sold eventually to the Seven Gables Book Shop. A much more substantial collection was that of Mrs. Edna Greenwood, the bulk of which, through a New York bookseller, went to a well-known mid-western collector. Mrs. Greenwood's *New England Primers* were bought by Seven Gables, and the copy of William Lily's Latin grammar with the youthful autograph of George Washington was bought by Goodspeed who had sold it to her many years before.

Though Winslow Homer's woodcuts in *Harper's Weekly* are well-known to collectors of his work, not many of them are aware that the first book in which any of his illustrations appear is a little juvenile, *Eventful History of Three Little Mice and How They Became Blind.* It was published in Boston in 1858 and it sold for "12 1/2 cts. plain" and "25 cts. colored." Homer is not the only name famous for other work whose first book was a juvenile. George Ade wrote two miniature books for the *Little Folks Library*. Thomas Bailey Aldrich is probably best remembered today for *The Story of a Bad Boy* but it is the only juvenile production among the many works of that eminent man of letters.

Edward Eggleston is best known as a pioneer of realistic fiction in this country, but his first literary publication was *Mr. Blake's Walking Stick: a Christmas Story for Boys and Girls.* Sinclair Lewis's first book was a story for boys, *Hike and the Aeroplane*. Amy Lowell's first appearance in a book (published when she was thirteen) was two fairy tales published anonymously in *Dream Drops*. Jacob Blanck was not only the compiler of *Peter Parley to Penrod* and editor of the monumental *Bibliography of American Literature*, but the author of two juveniles, *Jonathan and the Rainbow* and *The King and Noble Blacksmith*. The propaganda fiction of the indefatigable Upton Sinclair was preceded by a series of pseudonymous "Mark Mallory" and "Cliff Faraday" stories of Army and Navy life, clearly written for the juvenile market. Conversely, L. Frank Baum's first book was a how-to-do-it for poultry farmers, *The Book of Hamburgs, a brief Treatise upon mating, rearing and management of the different varieties of Hamburgs*, anticipating, by the way, Robert Frost's early contributions to the literature of hen-raising by nearly twenty years.

Baum's great classic, *The Wonderful Wizard of Oz* has always been a rarity in fine condition. Such a copy, presented by the illustrator W.W. Denslow to Charles Warren Stoddard at the time of publication, and also inscribed by the author, with an original drawing by Denslow, was offered in a Goodspeed catalogue in 1909. Half a century later, on the death of the original purchaser, the copy passed once more into Goodspeed's hands. On this second go around, it realized exactly three hundred times the earlier price. The same catalogue listed a copy of the first edition of *Tom Sawyer*, inscribed by the author, also to Stoddard, at the modest price of ten dollars.

Unlike the *Wizard of Oz, Tom Sawyer* never came back to us, and remains but a memory, though bodily it may be seen in the Lilly Library at the University of Indiana.

John Ruskin, after years of popular (and critical) neglect is once more fashionable with scholars and collectors. His first published book (the *Poems* of 1850 was privately printed) was a book for children, *The King of the Golden River*, a fairy story written in answer to a challenge from his fiancée in 1841. It was published with illustrations by Richard Doyle in 1851. C.E. Goodspeed, a life-long admirer of Ruskin, bought the original manuscript at the sale of Ruskin's library in 1930. The book is of some rarity: there was no copy of the first edition in the substantial Goodspeed collection in the Wellesley College library. A few years back the donor's son was delighted to be able to fill the gap.

The first two books in Blanck's *Peter Parley to Penrod, The Tales of Peter Parley about America*, 1827, and *The Little Scholar learning to Talk. A Picture Book for Rollo*, 1835, are both of legendary rarity. Of the first, the beginning volume in an almost interminable series of Peter Parley books, only three copies are recorded. As a measure of its extreme rarity I cite its inclusion in the catalogue of *A Society's Chief Joys*, Worcester, 1969, where the American Antiquarian Society's imperfect copy (wanting three leaves) is dignified with a reproduction of the title-page. An immaculate copy of this book, with the boyish autograph of a United States Senator turned up in a Rhode Island library which we bought years ago. *The Little Scholar*, the first Rollo book, is of even greater rarity. A copy of it which proved to be the only perfect copy of which there is a record was offered to us by a correspondent a few years later. It is now in the collection of the American Antiquarian Society.

Longfellow's *Tales of a Wayside Inn* is not always thought of as a book for children, though children for generations have learned the story of Paul Revere and his ride from the somewhat fictitious ballad commencing "Listen, my children and you shall hear Of the midnight ride of Paul Revere." People forget that the *Tales* contains the first printing of "The Children's Hour" in which the poet describes his three daughters "grave Alice, and laughing Allegra, and Edith with golden hair." Longfellow gave copies of the book to each of the three girls, inscribed merely with the name of the child and the date, in his hand. Through what strange accident, I will never know, Edith's copy was picked up for a dime in the sidewalk stall at Goodspeed's Milk Street Shop. The purchaser, embarrassed to offer it to us, sold it to another local bookseller, from whom I was fortunate to be able to buy it. It is now in Charlottesville.

In terms of absolute rarity, the first edition of *Little Women* is not particularly uncommon, but like most popular books for the young, fine copies are another matter. The finest one I have ever handled came from an old collection in the town of Bedford, Massachusetts, the library of a minister which had been kept shelved for years in an unheated room. Not only had the books been little read; when we saw them they were covered with a coating of dust an eighth of an inch thick. When this protective coating was blown away, the original covers appeared in virginal splendor, the gilt lettering shining like new.

Aldrich's *Story of a Bad Boy*, which came out a year later is equally rare in fine condition, while the large paper copies, of which only three survive, are unprocurable. The *Bad Boy* was a favorite of my own boy-hood and I still own one of the two fine copies that I have ever seen, the gift of a generous father on Christmas Day fifty-four years ago. *The Elm Island Stories* of the Reverend Elijah Kellogg had been the companions of his own boy-hood, and it was a disappointment to him that their spell failed to carry over to the next generation.

During the years, we have had our share of rare juveniles, including two copies of Mrs. Hale's *Poems for Our Children* (1830) in which "Mary's Little Lamb" was first collected; and most recently one of the two known copies (albeit very imperfect) of the first edition (1698) of Benjamin Harris's *The Holy Bible in Verse*, in a charming contemporary binding with blind-stamped panel showing an Indian hunting wildfowl with his bow and arrow.

To one looking back over half a century, it seems as if the supply of rarities in this field is drying up. But a little time is still left, and perhaps one of these days someone will drop in at 18 Beacon Street with a copy of *A New Gift for Children*, the first known non-biblical book for children, published in Boston about 1756. To date, the only known copy of the first edition is in the Huntington Library. The 1690 edition of the *New England Primer* is yet to turn up anywhere!

* * * * * * * * *

LITERATI IN THE BOOKSHOP

BOSTON was formerly one of the best sources of supply that any antiquarian bookseller could wish for. This was due to the very considerable number of old family accumulations to be expected in an area which had such a prominent role in the early history of the United States, and to the nineteenth century flowering of literature in New England. I have referred earlier to the wealth of association books from Lowell's library. Another writer, a favorite among collectors, whose books have a way of turning up locally is Henry Adams.

We have, I believe, had as many copies of the privately printed editions of *The Education of Henry Adams* and the even more elusive *Mont Saint Michel and Chartres* as anyone in the trade. We have also had on occasion copies of *Esther* published in 1884 under the pseudonym of "Frances Snow Compton." *Esther* like Adams's earlier novel *Democracy* was published anonymously by Henry Holt as one of a series of novels by American authors. Only 1000 copies were printed and even this small edition failed to sell out. It is today very rare. The copy I remember was offered in the mimeographed catalogue of a small South End dealer (I have mentioned him in another connection earlier in my narrative, but shall not identify him otherwise). My previous experience with this gentleman was of such a nature that I was embarrassed to call him on the telephone in which case I should have to identify myself, so I took a cab to the indicated address and paid cash for the book. It seemed unnecessary to ask for a trade discount on the posted price of $1.35.

I had hardly got back to the shop when Richard Wormser called me from New York, complaining that Bostonians got up too early in the morning. He wheedled the book out of me for $100.00 (remember this was many years ago). He sold half of his interest to the newly formed Seven Gables Book Shop. It was resold shortly thereafter to the also newly formed partnership known as Baker & Brooks for $315.00. With them it hung fire for a year or so. What it finally realized I cannot say, but it must have been about five hundred times what I had paid for it originally.

Despite the eminence of the Adams family in the history (and literature) of our country, its members have on occasion been treated with something less than the reverence to which they are entitled. I forbear requoting the entertaining squib at the expense of Charles Francis Adams, Jr., which may be found in *Yankee Bookseller* (pp. 86-7), but the following quatrain, beginning with a quotation from the *New England Primer*, which the late M.A. DeWolfe Howe wrote in his copy of the *Education*, is perhaps worthy of preservation:

> At Adams's fall
> We sinned all
> And ever since that maladroit beginning
> Against the Adamses the world's been sinning!

Howe must have read these lines to Gamaliel Bradford, for in the same copy is laid the typescript of some verses by Bradford, with a note "send me your verses, so that I may put them in my 'Education'."

A collection of such spontaneous epigrams written as marginalia could be very entertaining. My favorite is the one pencilled by George Santayana in a copy of T.S. Eliot's *The Use of Poetry* which I bought years ago from Santayana's secretary, then retired in Sussex:

> How very virtuous I should be
> If Eliot had created me.
> But how deserving of the rod
> I am descended from the hand of God!

During the later years of his life, Edmund Wilson was a frequent if somewhat irregular customer both at Milk Street and at Beacon Street, where he particularly fancied the folio lithographs from Audubon's *Quadrupeds*. His taste ran to the smaller rodents: the mice, moles and rats, which up to that time sold at very low prices — many as little as three or four dollars a plate. Despite his reputation for rudeness, I always found him an entertaining talker. On one occasion he remarked on an unusual collection of (more or less) contemporary first editions which we had just purchased. "If you think this is a good lot, you should see mine." I expressed interest, but he continued that he wouldn't sell during his life. "However," he continued, "I am leaving my books to my son, and will suggest that he call on you when the time comes."

Though the aggregate value of the collection we were discussing was not very great, I thought it would be fun to get out a catalogue of them, which I did. The Nimrod Press produced a distinctively styled booklet, and the result was predictably successful. I felt that it was another demonstration of the flexibility in style on which we have always prided ourselves.

It was about the same time, when we were planning to issue our five hundredth catalogue that my friend Terry Baker at Houghton Mifflin asked me whether I would like a copy of a little pamphlet poem by Edmund Wilson which Terry had produced on short notice at the author's request. The poem, entitled *The White Sand for Elena December 10, 1950* had been written for the occasion of the Wilsons's fourth wedding anniversary. A few days before the occasion Terry had been asked to produce a printed copy. Explaining that such instant production was more than the mammoth Riverside Press could be asked to turn out overnight, he undertook to set the poem up himself and print a dozen copies on the hand-lever platen press then located in the basement of the Fenn School in Concord.

Of course, I was delighted with the gift, but asked whether I might instead buy it to add spice to our forthcoming catalogue. It developed that Terry had been permitted to keep three of the little

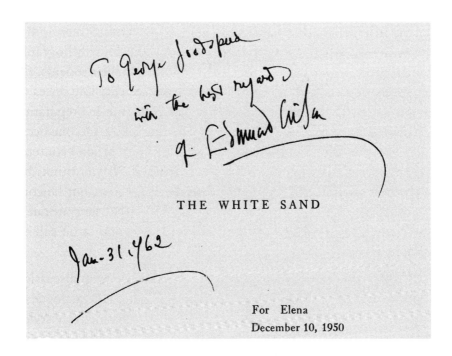

THE WHITE SAND

For   Elena
December 10, 1950

edition for himself, so I had one for my own use and two to supply to customers from the catalogue.

The next time Wilson was in, I solicited his autograph inscription in my own copy. Three months later, when he was eyeing another little batch of Audubon's animals, he offered me a copy of *White Sand* from his own library in trade. To this I agreed. As it turned out, this copy also I had to keep personally, for he not only inscribed it to me, but he had made manuscript corrections and one substantial revision in the text.

A few years later, after Wilson's death, I did indeed hear from his son about the disposal of his father's library, and accompanied by my wife, I drove to Orleans and spent a couple of very interesting hours with the books. The quantity (25,000 volumes, I'd guess) was staggering, and I explained that it would be quite impossible to put a figure on the collection on the basis of such a cursory inspection. The little section devoted to presentation copies from contemporary poets was exciting but not of very large value. The complete run of inscribed first editions of Wilson's Princeton contemporary F. Scott Fitzgerald was of course sensational. Since the books were not immediately for sale, it was left that when they were, I might return and do a thorough valuation. A year later when a sale was imminent, difficulties arose and I was not permitted a second look. It is disappointing to lose a purchase under competition, but to fail without having a chance to bid is downright frustration.

Robert Frost was among the great contemporaries not represented on Wilson's shelves of inscribed copies, though to tell the truth, Frost and Wilson were not at all friendly, and during the celebrated row between De Voto and Wilson in the columns of the *Saturday Review*, he was passively on De Voto's side. My own acquaintance with Frost had been through John Kohn, one of my younger contemporaries in the book trade.

In the early 'thirties John Kohn, after taking his master's degree at Harvard in 1930 and serving a brief apprenticeship with the Argosy Book Stores in New York, had set up in business for himself as the Collector's Book Shop. We early developed a friendship which continued until John's death in 1976. He had, at the beginning of his bookselling career, become a specialist in contemporary poetry, particularly Frost and Robinson, and had besides a very fine personal Frost collection.

It was he who introduced me to Frost in 1938 not long after Mrs. Frost's death. Robert Frost was then living in an apartment at 88 Mt. Vernon Street just opposite Louisburg Square. I don't remember much of the conversation, except that our host talked at length about his wife, and her attitude towards his work, about which, he said, she had been possessively jealous, resenting, almost, the public acclaim which it had finally earned. This was a theme to which he often returned later, but at the time this objective discussion with a stranger seemed to me oddly lacking in reserve.

Above the mantelpiece was a framed lithograph of the well at Bolonchen from Catherwood's folio *Views of Ancient Monuments in Central America*. The well, at the bottom of a cave 210 feet below the surface, is reached by a wide ladder on which natives laden with buckets of water toil upwards towards a seemingly unattainable summit. I remarked on the dramatic effect of the print, and Frost said that he had bought it from us as a portrayal of the utmost in human toil. If I am not mistaken he still had it when he moved to the house on Brewster Street in Cambridge, and it remained there until he died.

Over the next few years we met occasionally, usually, I think, at the St. Botolph Club, of which he had been made an honorary member, though his visits there were infrequent. It was at one of these meetings, I suppose, that I asked him whether he would care to come to our house in Concord for dinner. Dinner in the country meant spending the night, for Frost's evenings were always late ones. I think his greatest pleasure was in conversation in small groups — conversations which were more like monologues, and this particular evening wound up at one o'clock in the morning, our guest retiring at that hour, I am sure, out of consideration for his sleepy host and hostess.

In the course of the evening I mentioned Clarence King's *Mountaineering in the Sierra Nevada*, one of the unrecognized masterpieces in American literature. I had first read of this neglected classic in Van Wyck Brooks's *New England: Indian Summer*, a couple of years earlier. Curiously, for a Westerner and outdoorsman, Frost had never heard of King's book. When we all went up to bed, he took my copy with him to read. I never saw the book again, a circumstance which I never resented, recognizing, I suppose, a sort of bibliophilic *droit de seigneur*. My sense of deprivation, moreover, was tempered by the happy discovery a little later, of a copy of the rare large paper edition and a presentation copy to boot, lurking innocently on the shelves of our Milk Street shop.

I have never had much use for association copies inscribed by request and I know Frost was constantly importuned for his autograph, but it seemed appropriate that we have some souvenir of the visit. A framed copy of the broadside printing by Dard Hunter, Jr., of Frost's *A Considerable Speck* hung on our living room wall, and the

By permission of the Houghton Library, Harvard University

Reviewing Goodspeed's guest register at a staff luncheon (left to right: John Farquharson, Sr., Ivis J. [Mrs. George T.] Goodspeed, Robert Frost, Arnold Silverman, Gordon Banks)

next morning I asked him to inscribe it for us. As he was in the process of doing so, our young daughter Carol (then three and a half) queried "What are you writing, Mr. Frost?" Replying that he was writing her parents' names on the poem he added "Perhaps I should write out a little poem for you. Would you like that?" Embarrassed, the young lady took refuge in the defensive negative "No." Such was the vanity of genius that he was put off by the instinctive rebuff of a child, and I am certain that thereafter nothing could have induced him to produce the "little poem."

Two years later, in 1944, I had a call from Robert asking my wife and myself to dinner at his house in Cambridge, in honor of Lawrance Thompson. Thompson was an old friend of mine, whom I had met years before at Carroll Wilson's. In the years before the war he had stayed frequently at our house in Concord while he was at work on his *Young Longfellow*, commuting to Craigie House in Cambridge where the Longfellow archives were kept. He had early been an admirer of Frost's poetry and his first book was *Robert Frost, A Chronological Study*, published at Wesleyan in 1936. Frost's home was half a spacious two-family house with three adjoining rooms, front to back, the kitchen at the rear. Our host greeted us at the door, apologizing for the abscence of the guest of honor, who had been called back to New York on Navy business. Frost's daughter, Leslie, had come up from Washington to hostess the occasion. Frost knew of our relationship with Thompson, and may have asked us for that reason, but I doubt the party had really been planned in his honor. More likely it was held to pay off the many social obligations at one time, for the company was a large and varied one, as if the selection of the guest list had been made at random. We found a few acquaintances and a few faces that looked familiar, but many were strangers to us and apparently to each other. The informal buffet had hardly been served, some of the guests standing, some sitting on the floor, and a few in chairs, when an air raid alert was sounded. Frost had never taken the trouble to have the house properly blacked out, so the assembly was stopped in its tracks so to speak. The sensation of being plunged suddenly into absolute darkness in a group of relative strangers was an eerie one, but conversation of a sort was possible and everyone behaved themselves. When the lights went on at last, Robert went back to the kitchen and brought out some bottles of whiskey and as many as could be accommodated sat with him around the kitchen table for more talk.

We always thought of Frost as the personification of the rugged New England virtues of prudence and responsibility, but he was in fact, singularly casual about money matters. Happening on one of our catalogues late in 1945, he called me with a rather long order (not that the amount was large). It was a mixed lot of minor books, mostly in nineteenth century American literature. This little transaction was a minor source of embarrassment to me because for years it went unpaid. We could have dropped the small amount off to profit and loss, but felt (mistakenly, as I now realize) that Frost's independent spirit would resent having us do so. After a lapse of several years, probably under the prodding of Mrs. Morrison, the bill was paid.

In the summer of 1949, the Thompsons invited us to spend a couple of nights with them in Ripton, Vermont. Larry was teaching at Breadloaf and Frost had lent the Thompsons his Ripton farmhouse for the summer. Frost walked over the hill for dinner one evening and the after-dinner-talk was useful to Larry, who could sit off in a corner and Boswellize without being involved in the conversation. In what way Reed Powell's name came up, I don't recall, but Frost remarked that Powell had been up visiting a few days earlier, and in the course of a walk over the hills had said, "You're not really a Vermonter. After all you were born in San Francisco, and spent most of your life in New Hampshire. You're just a bastard Vermonter." Alluding to the sharp tongue for which Professor Powell was notorious, Frost replied "Better a bastard Vermonter than a Vermont bastard."

Apart from a few poems appearing in the *Lawrence High School Bulletin*, the first of Robert Frost's poems to appear in print was the *Class Hymn* in the Lawrence High School Graduation program, July 1, 1892. This leaflet was mentioned, but not described in Clymer and Green's *Bibliography* and I think that no copy had turned up until 1961 (or thereabouts) when a young man living in Lawrence found an example tucked in a book that he had picked up at a rummage sale. It is axiomatic that when one copy of a rarity turns up, another is likely to follow.

Frost, then in the popular limelight partly because of his recent participation in the Kennedy Inauguration, was guest of honor at the High School's anniversary celebration in January, 1962. The event got extensive press coverage, and in the newspaper accounts were listed the surviving classmates of 1892. We wrote these survivors (I think there were three) enquiring for copies of the program. One charming old lady wrote that she had one which she would be glad to sell "because I would like to have the poem passed on to posterity." A little later my friend Bill Jewell, whose father had been a close friend of Frost's produced three more copies. As far as I am aware, these five copies, all of which thus passed through our hands, are all that are known to survive.

From the Jewell collection also came some odd numbers of the *High School Bulletin* of Lawrence containing the first printings of some of Frost's earlier poems, and the original promissory note signed "Robert Lee Frost" given to Ernest C. Jewell in 1902 acknowledging a loan of $675.00 advanced to help Frost set up his hen farm in Derry, New Hampshire. For some time I kept the unpaid note so that Frost might not be embarrassed. Eventually I made a present of it to Waller Barrett who in turn gave it to the University of Virginia to be kept under seal until Frost's death. It is reproduced in the recently published catalogue of the Barrett Frost collection at Charlottesville.

A few weeks before the second leaflet turned up, Frost was our guest at one of the shop's regular weekly staff luncheons. The coolness arising from the aftermath of the Russian journey was still in the future and Frost's admiration for Kennedy (whom he said he had advised to be "more Irish than Harvard") was still in the ascendent. We produced no books to be autographed (other than the bookshop's guest register), a circumstance which I think disappointed him.

The Russian trip itself had a curious bibliographical sequel. In March, 1963, F.B. Adams, who had accompanied Frost on this much publicized journey, read a paper "To Russia with Frost" before the Club of Odd Volumes. The late William A. Jackson then President of the Odd Volumes expressed a hope that the club might be permitted to publish it.

Nothing came of the suggestion immediately, but when the talk was repeated at the Grolier Club later, Joseph Blumenthal asked whether he might do an edition for that club. Adams said that he

ALICE IN BOTOLPHLAND

By

DAVID McCORD

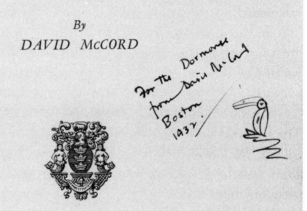

Printed for the St. Botolph Club

BOSTON · 1932

had given the Odd Volumes the refusal of publication rights, where-upon Blumenthal offered to print the edition very reasonably if he might have copies for himself. Accordingly an edition of 500 was published, ostensibly by the Club. Actually the author got 100 copies, Holt (Frost's publisher) 25, and Blumenthal 125 (approximately). This left 250 copies for the Club of Odd Volumes. Sixty, however, were damaged in transit. Blumenthal reprinted enough sheets to make up the deficit. This involved reprinting the illustrations which had originally been printed gratis by Harold Hugo at the Meriden Gravure Company. For the reprint Hugo made a small charge. At long last, however, the reprint was damaged in the bindery and never was issued.

In the meantime, the members of the Odd Volumes showed no great interest in the book and a number of copies were left over. John Kohn and I, as members, eventually bought the remainder between us.

An intimate of Frost in his younger days was David McCord. The two met in 1924 when the younger poet was three years out of college. McCord's first book of essays, *Oddly Enough*, published in 1926, was the first publication of the firm of Washburn & Thomas, a pseudonymous style composed of the middle names of its partners David W. Bailey and David T. Pottinger. Bailey was an old friend of mine and a classmate of McCord, and it was at about this time that McCord and I became friends. It was through his kindness that I became a member of the St. Botolph Club in 1931, and starred as the dormouse in *Alice in Botolphland*, a pantomime with narration by its author, produced at the Twelfth Night revels in 1932. The skit appeared in pamphlet form with illustrations, including a photograph of the tea-party scene with Edward Weeks as Alice, Lovell Thompson as the March Hare, William A.B. Kirkpatrick as the Mad Hatter, and Goodspeed as a very timid Dormouse.

The innumerable ephemeral printings of McCord's occasional verse will someday be the despair of his bibliographers. In the print-ing of one or two of these I must acknowledge some share of the responsibility. I am proud of my small part in one of them. On January 25, 1965, the day of Winston Churchill's death, the front page of *The Boston Globe* carried an elegiac ode *In Memory of Sir Winston Churchill* by David McCord. It began:

> The long count-down is over: he is gone
> The world that died this morning, eight plus
> something, London time, swept most of us
> with it — who will not remember? Presently
> there is another world, no better against his
> dogged hope, no worse perhaps against our naked
> fears. So we continue, warned of extinguished
> lights along the breakwater, pulling switches
> voiding giant valves because we gauge not
> much in sorrow worth the hurling into space.

I found the poem very moving and asked the author if I might print a small edition of it to give to members of The Club of Odd Volumes on the following Saturday, which chanced to be the day chosen for Churchill's state funeral. We arranged to have the newspaper setting reproduced in facsimile and printed by offset in an edition of ninety copies for members of the club. Union rules prohibited mechanical reproduction of the newsprint, but this was got around by having the poem reset in linotype. It was David who did all of the work at the *Globe* and obtained the paper's permission to reprint. I contributed only the idea, and the small cost of production.

A little book *About Boston* an expansion of a series of radio broadcasts by McCord appeared under the Doubleday imprint in 1948. It was illustrated with head and tail pieces from drawings by the author, who also contributed a watercolor of Beacon Hill from across the Charles River, which was used to decorate the dust jacket. Since the little view did not appear inside, the book is incomplete, as sometimes happens, without the jacket. The back of the wrapper was given up to a series of commendatory blurbs by friends of the author: H.M. Tomlinson, M.A. DeWolfe Howe, Ralph Lowell, Ernest

Hooten and Charles E. Goodspeed. The book went through four printings before it was taken over, about 1952 by Little Brown, who issued a page for page reprint. The blurbs on the dust jacket were replaced by quotations from book reviews by Ferris Greenslet, Edward Weeks, Mason Wade, Joseph Henry Jackson and N.J. O'Conor. In 1953, when the American Bar Association held its Diamond Jubilee Convention in Boston, the Massachusetts and Boston Bar Associations brought out an abridged version for presentation to the visiting lawyers. It reprinted the first ten and the last of the essays in the original, and retained the colored illustration on the front jacket. It contained a Foreword by a leader of the Boston Bar devoted largely to an account of the part played by John Adams as lawyer for the British soldiers involved in the Boston Massacre. As the account contains three substantive misstatements of fact in connection with the incident, it is as well that it does not appear in subsequent printings of the book.

The complete text was reprinted once more in 1973, this time as a paperback, with a photographic view of the new skyscraped city from the same vantage point, replacing the McCord drawing.

The old blurbs by Tomlinson, Greenslet, Weeks and Jackson, somewhat abridged, appear on the back wrapper, with a new one by another Goodspeed.

It was late in the winter (March 11, to be exact) of 1944 that Louis Auchincloss, who had been an occasional customer since his Groton school-days stopped in and bought a set of Jane Austen first editions. It was in a good, sound, midnineteenth century half binding, though without half-titles. He was pleased to find it, he said, because he was on his way to his ship (an L.S.T.) for duty in the South Pacific and Miss Austen was perfect reading matter for the voyage. I remarked that there was something incongruous about Jane Austen first editions on an L.S.T., but he said that he liked the format and would enjoy reading the novels as they first appeared. He paid for the set and gave his Fleet P.O. address in New York. The books were duly dispatched, and a year later I had a letter from

Louis, now returned, inquiring what had happened to the set. The books had been insured and I reimbursed him. We have both speculated since about what did happen. We have come to the conclusion that the set is still reposing in some Navy warehouse, and may turn up years from now at some government auction sale. Where it will most certainly fetch more than the $195.00 it was sold for in 1943.

* * * * * * * * *

THE INDIAN GIFT

THE OLDEST organization of antiquarian booksellers in the
English-speaking world is the Antiquarian Booksellers Association
(International) founded in London in 1906. Though the word "international" was incorporated in the name from the beginning, and the
Association has always welcomed members from overseas, it is essen-
tially British in character and membership. We must be one of the
oldest members; at least the date on our membership certficate is
1907. It was not until 1949 that an American association called
imaginatively "The Antiquarian Booksellers' Association of America"
was chartered with headquarters in New York. The term "antiquarian" by the way had previously enjoyed little currency in this country.
It has, however, the great virtue of inclusiveness, so that the smallest
dealer in second hand books (who inevitably has a "rare" book on
occasion) is on common ground with his *confrère* who handles only
expensive rarities.

Both of these organizations are now associated with those of
Europe and Asia through membership in the International League,
and because of this and the proliferation of travel by jet aircraft, the
trade has taken on a truly global character, and a bookseller will find
that he has a friend and colleague in almost every city in the western
world.

Nevertheless, our dealings with the Orient (outside of Japan)
have been infrequent. It was on a Saturday morning three years ago,
that there arrived in the mail a letter on the letterhead of a firm of

"New & Antiquarian Book Sellers, Direct Importers & Exporters" of Ahmedabad in India. The letter read in part:

> You will be happy to know that we have received a very big lot of old books (mostly of Eighteenth centuries) on different subjects. We are sending you by separate post our list of books to you and you will find our prices are very reasonable. We are confident that you will favour us with your valued order.
>
> We are dealing in this line for the last seven years and able to establish business contacts with various parties throughout the world because of our efficient service, excellent bindings of good books and competitive prices. It will be pleasure for us to enter into business dealing with you, too.
>
> We shall be glad if you will favour us with your esteemed order as soon as possible.

On Saturday mornings we are thinly staffed, and it was the better part of an hour before I came to the little batch of catalogues which form a substantial portion of every bookseller's morning post. When I got the catalogues at last, I found two lists from our Indian friend. One of them was a "List of Books, on Genealogy, General Subjects . . . etc. . . . in Ready Stock." The other was entitled "Books on Travel . . . etc.," also "In Ready Stock."

The lot of books on genealogy, which by the way was devoted as much to books on topography and travel as to family history, included Acosta's *History of the East and West Indies*, London, 1604, at $30.00; Adair's *History of the American Indians*, 1775, at $13.00; Malton's *Picturesque Tour Through the Cities of London and Westminster illustrated with Views in Aquatinta*, two volumes folio, $20.00; Carey and Lea's *American Atlas, . . .* consisting of 53 charts (coloured), $30.00; and eighty-six others similarly priced.

The second list was even more titillating. It commenced with the *Arrival and Entertainment of the Embassador Alkaid Yaurar Ben*

98

Abdallu, with his associate Mr. Robert Blake, from Muley Mohammed Sheque, Emperor of Morrocco . . . London, 1637 at $20.00, and continued on through Bossu's *Travels Through Louisiana*, 1771 at $18.00, Bradford's *Sketches . . . in Portugal and Spain*, 56 colored plates, folio, $18.00; Dampier's *Collection of Voyages*, 4 volumes, 1729, $30.00; Eden's *The History of Travayle in the West and East Indies* . . . London 1577, $20.00; and Hakluyt's *Voyages*, 1598-1599-1600, three volumes, $38.00.

The sum of the books on the list averaged at somewhere around five per cent of the value of the books. Each list bore the warning: "only one copy each in stock — Rush your order: C.W.O. Always: Free Delivery by Sea Mail. Invoice by Air."

The prices were so ridiculously low that naturally I suspected a hoax, and I called Dick Wormser, who had more connections in far-off lands than anyone I knew. He, I thought, would also have received the lists. Being in the country, however, his mail wasn't delivered on Saturdays. He came up with the suggestion that we buy the contents of both lists jointly, and that I cable $200.00 advance payment on the collection. I found that you can't cable money on Saturdays, but I did wire an order for the lot, which was followed the next week by the promised downpayment.

On Monday Wormser called. Now he had a list — one even more remarkable. It was primarily natural history, with editions of Gould's ornithological works, also at bargain prices. A few days later, it developed that our friend Peter Decker had had the two lists that had been sent to me. Eventually we all received courteous letters of acknowledgement from India. The final letter reaching me wound up "we shall send you the books in due course."

An inquiry through our bank yielded the information that our Indian colleague was "reported to be respectable but possessed of very small means."

Three months later another colleague of ours, Steve Weissman in New York, got a printed letter which I reproduce as follows:

INDERJIT & CO.
NEW & ANTIQUARIAN BOOK SELLERS
DIRECT IMPORTERS & EXPORTERS

492/A, SINDHI COLONY, SARDARNAGAR TOWNSHIP, AHMEDABAD.
(India)

Our Ref. No. E/1101/2
Date Feb. 21, 1975
M/S. Ximenes: Rare Books,
U.S.A.

Dear Sirs,

As you are perhaps aware that we are one of the leading Antiquarian Book sellers in India. We have been serving almost all over the world to the Universities, Institutions, Book sellers and Individuals by despatching books for the last seven years. We have been maintaining our relations very nicely with our foreign buyers. We have also been appreciated by many foreign buyers in this respect for our good services.

It is our desire to bring into your kind notice that 'Unfortunately' on January 18, 1975 divastating fire broke out in our office due to 'ELECTRIC SHORT CIRCUIT' and the total loss has taken place more than Rs. 25,000/- (TWENTY FIVE THOUSANDS) The collection of very precious and Antiquarian books have burnt off due to unexpected fire we have been totally ruined and still we are very much interested to continue our organisation.

It is therefore requested to help us to re-establish our organisation by way of donating. Whatever donation you will give us will be refundable to you by despatching the books of your choice. We have very nice sources in India to get the very rare books. We hope that you will look into the matter very minutely and will do the needful

For your immediate reference, we enclose herewith the copy of the news published in 'INDIAN EXPRESS' on January 18 and January 21, 1975. We hope with your kind and generous help we will be able to serve you better in future.

Awaiting your generous donation, we remain

Very Truly Yours.

For **Inderjit & Co.**

(Inderjit)
Proprietor
Enclosed: As above

100

The enclosure was a news item from an Ahmedabad paper of January 18 confirming the fact of the fire. Were the books destroyed in this fire? If so, our Mr. Inderjit had kept them in his possession for two months after receiving payment. Anyhow, we had, though unintentionally, through our gullibility contributed in advance to his fortunes.

The mystery was never cleared up. One thing is certain: the books were there. The man's descriptions were too thorough and accurate to be fabrications. And the nature of the collection was entirely consistent with such a library as might have been left by an old British army officer or civil servant. As far as I am aware, Decker, Wormser and ourselves were the only booksellers in this country, at least, to get the lists, and the books themselves never seem to have surfaced. The most plausible explanation is that the books were there but that our correspondent was still negotiating for their purchase from a third party. Had either Goodspeed, Wormser or Decker been twenty years younger, one of us would have hopped a plane for the remote Indian city and found out for ourselves.

Wormser's suggestion of the two hundred dollar gamble was typical of his imagination which, not infrequently, I am sure led him into similar speculations, many of which paid off. In any event, the odds in this particular instance were sufficiently attractive. He was addicted to the bad pun and, after the incident had passed, he sent a check for his half of the venture enclosed in this note:

INDIGENT & CO.
Ah Me How Bad?
Nov. 5 1974
Goodspeed & Co.

Dear Sirs:
    I enclose $100, my share of the Indian Giving.

Yours
Richard S. Wormser

Perhaps the books still remain in some remote country house library, waiting for an enterprising bookseller from the West to unearth them.

* * * * * * * * *

AUDUBON

I HAVE mentioned before the term "breaker" for books frequently broken up for sale by the leaf, or, more usually, for the illustrations which are sold as prints. The most famous and the most expensive today, of course, is the great folio edition of Audubon's *Birds of America*. But the prints from this great work were not always so highly esteemed, and it was not until comparatively recent times that complete sets were broken up for the illustrations.

Odd volumes, however, came on the market occasionally, and, we were among the first to exploit the prints in this way. Indeed, as recently as fifty years ago our supply of them was so ample that we were able to consign quantities to others for sale without seriously depleting our own stock. The Scribner Bookstore in New York and the Henderson County Historical Society in Kentucky were two of our principal outlets.

As early as 1905 we were able to catalogue at one time nearly two hundred of the bird plates at the extremely modest prices then prevailing. The Snowy Owl, for example, was listed at twenty dollars; the Columbia Jay at twelve dollars and a half; the Great Blue Heron at twenty; and the others in proportion at prices not more than one per cent of what they fetch today.

We have never broken a complete set of this monumental work. A few months after I came to the shop, we catalogued the fine set from Amy Lowell's library for $3500 (an advance of only $500.00 over what we had asked in 1903) and not long after a remarkably fine set bound in full levant by Sanford the old Boston binder, found no

103

buyers at about the same price. Sanford used to tell of the many months it took him to find skins large enough for the binding.

The work was originally published by subscription, and some subscribers, for one reason or another, allowed their subscriptions to lapse. As a result, portions of the first two volumes occasionally turn up in the hands of descendants of the original subscribers. One such lot came to light in New Jersey in 1950. It was in February of that year that I had been in New York and called on David Randall, then manager of Scribner's rare book department. In the course of my visit, he picked up a letter lying on his desk, waved it casually and remarked that it was from a woman nearby who had the first hundred and five plates from the Audubon. The prints were totally untrimmed and first states throughout. "I have offered $4,000" he said "but the owner has made no decision." The letter, which of course he did not let me see closely, was on a characteristic blue note paper. I should naturally have liked to have a chance to bid on the prints. When I got back to Boston, I found on my desk what was clearly the counterpart of the one Dave had waved in front of me. I called the owner of the plates, made an appointment to see her the next day, went back to New York on the night train, and proceeded down to the New Jersey suburb. It was not difficult to come to terms with the owner at $4,500. Bookselling is a very talky business, and the temptation to blab is sometimes irresistible.

Getting the heavy, bulky prints back to Boston presented some logistical problems, but I managed by taking a taxi to New York, where the big portfolio was deposited in the Harvard Club's check-room while I had lunch, and a ten dollar tip to a Pullman porter on the old "Knickerbocker Limited" got me permission to get it into the club car.

Eleven years later a lot of the prints in the same mint condition appeared in Toronto. There were a hundred and sixty of them. Miss Jarvis, who had just become proprietor of Dora Hood's Book Room, had offered the collection in a catalogue at $17,500 but found no buyer, and the late Harry Newman, not then as keen on these prints as he later became, called them to my attention. I called Miss Jarvis and we agreed on a net price of $15,000.

My wife and I drove to Toronto arriving late on the third of July. The next morning, having bought the prints, we started back home, my purchase in the trunk. Crossing the border at Buffalo, we found the customs house lightly staffed because of the Fourth of July holiday. The inspector wanted to know how long we had been in Canada and whether we were bringing anything back. Only some old prints, I replied. Were they for my own use? No, they were bought for the company by whom I was employed. He was about to wave us through when he asked how much I had paid for the engravings.

A truthful answer to the last question cost us an hour and a half. The prints were not dutiable, as I knew, but I couldn't find the pertinent paragraph in the thick volume of custom regulations. When the matter was finally cleared up, it became necessary to locate a customs broker to put up a bond. (The brokers were taking the holiday off.)

Now we have to buy Audubons in small lots. The last complete set to be sold, in indifferent condition, brought $247,000, and has now been broken up.

A similar explosion has occurred in the prices of folio lithographs in the *Viviparous Quadrupeds of North America* after drawings by Audubon and his son, issued between 1845 and 1848 and followed by a second edition in 1855. The first edition published in three volumes is greatly superior to the second. When I entered the business we had a stack of these three folio volumes standing three feet high on the floor of the shop. We asked a hundred and fifty dollars a set for them and they moved slowly. Eighteen years ago, sets were bringing three thousand and last year one brought twenty thousand at auction in New York.

* * * * * * * * *

105

BOSTON VIEWS

FROM THE DESK at which I am sitting I look out on the facade of what Bostonians consider the most beautiful state Capitol, if not the most beautiful public building in America. And on the wall at my left elbow hangs the earliest print in which this noble example of American architecture is shown.

Of the less successful reproductive engravings executed by Sidney L. Smith for Charles E. Goodspeed is that entitled "The Boston Troops, as reviewed on President Adams's birth day on the Common by his Honr. Lieut. Governor Gill & Maj. Genl. Elliott, under the command of Brigadier Genl. Winslow; also a view of the new State House &c. &c."

This small (the pictorial surface measures 7½ x 9¼ inches) mezzotint was issued as a folding frontispiece to the first number of a short-lived magazine, *The Columbian Phenix and Boston Review* which ran from January to July 1800. The rather weak and washed-out appearance of Smith's engraving may have been due to his lack of experience in the technique of mezzotint engraving, but it seems to me more likely that he was working from a weak impression of the original.

The scene depicted is a charming one. The newly-completed state house of Charles Bulfinch flanked by the old beacon to the northeast and the Hancock house to the west, sits in the background. On the Common, in front of it, several companies of militia are deployed, while in the foreground, various groups of civilians are engaged in promenading on what must have been an unusually clement day (the date was October 30). One little group is gathered around a tavern table with tankards while another surrounds what appears to be a dice game. Seated before the game are a couple in embrace while a drover, with his whip standing by, scratches his head either in wonder or perplexity. In the middle of the Common the firing of a cannon seems to attract little attention from the populace.

The publication for which this engraving was made is not an uncommon one: the *Union List of Serials* locates forty-one files. A census of the institutions where these files are located, however, indicates that the frontispiece is almost invariably wanting. Indeed, a file in the New York Public Library seems to be the only one in which it is present.

I had never seen an original of this print until a couple of years ago when one was brought in to us by a local dealer in antiques. Unlike Smith's re-engraving, it is a strong impression, printed in warm sepia. It has been folded twice, a clear evidence that it was once in a copy of the magazine.

The great rarity of this little print can hardly be, and indeed is not, due entirely to chance. A note appearing in the February number of the *Phenix* read:

> THE Editor of the Columbian Phenix is extremely mortified and unhappy, in being reduced to the necessity of apologizing to a great portion of his Subscribers, for the omission of the Frontispiece described in page 7th of this work. A very liberal sum was given to the Engraver, to finish the Plate in a style of excellence; but he has executed the Engraving so ineffectually, that it will not answer the required purpose, and is now altogether useless. The Editor confidently presumes, that a generous and discerning Public will not be disposed to blame him for the unfaithfulness of another, whose want of skill or duty he could not detect, until the evil was beyond reparation.

Note the expression above "he has executed the engraving so ineffectually that it . . . is now altogether useless."

As a matter of fact, the print is, for the period, very well executed and one of which any publisher at the time might well have been proud. It is more likely that because the copper was too soft, or the plate too lightly engraved, the plate wore out after a very few impressions had been pulled, hence "is *now* altogether useless." This might account for the appearance of Smith's engraving if he had had to use a late impression for his original. The name of the engraver, or indeed the artist of this print has never been determined.

Rare though it is, the Boston Common mezzotint has long been known. The two or three copies that we know of doubtless owe their survival to the circumstances that they appeared in a periodical. What is more a subject of wonderment is the number of engravings that hitherto unknown continue to appear for the first time. The famous Bonner plan of Boston in its many states furnishes several instances of this.

This map, or plan of the town of Boston, which first appeared in 1722 enjoys the distinction of being the earliest city plan to be engraved in the colonies. The copper plate on which it was engraved remained in existence for many years, and it was altered continually to reflect the growth and changes of the town. Nine distinct editions of the map have survived, and of these nine, seven are known to exist in but a single example.

During the last half century, four examples of the map in its various incarnations have passed through our hands. Two of these four represent states known by no other copies. Of these two, one, dated 1760 was sold to the Houghton Library at Harvard in 1943.

The second of them turned up only recently in England, whence we acquired it. It might be assumed that after the passage of more than a quarter of a millenium no new states would be found. But this newly discovered example is evidence that hitherto unknown specimens and even editions will continue to appear as long as there are antiquarians on the look-out for them. This newly discovered state, which I shall call the fourth differs from its predecessor only in the addition of one building on the plan with its corresponding reference in the *Explanation* below. Whether Dewing, the engraver, or Bonner and Price, the publishers, were endowed with sufficient prescience to be aware of the future significance in history of the newly depicted structure must be a matter of conjecture, but the only change in the edition of the map is the inclusion of a representation of Christ Church, now usually known as the Old North, which was erected in 1723.

By all odds the most significant engraved view of a New England college in the early eighteenth century is the familiar large representation of *A Prospect of the Colleges in New England* after a drawing by William Burgis, known in its first state only by an impression at the Massachusetts Historical Society. The same plate somewhat altered was issued in 1743, and four impressions of this state have survived. I have argued elsewhere (*M.H.S. Proceedings*, LXXIII, 25-6) that an intermediate state may have been issued in 1731. If a formerly unknown state of the Bonner plan can be discovered in 1976, who is to say that a new state of the Burgis Harvard may not yet be found?

As a portrayer of American life in the nineteenth century, Winslow Homer had few equals. One aspect of the local scene which seems to have had a particular fascination for him was ice skating, a favorite pastime when Homer was making his reputation. A writer in *Ballou's Pictorial*, describing a woodcut by Homer in the issue for March 12, 1859, commented "the enthusiasm for skating this year has amounted to a mania. We have heard of old ladies, who, to illustrate the truth of the maxim 'tis never to late to learn' have commenced skating at the age of sixty-five . . ."

A charming folio lithograph published by Bufford a year earlier is almost certainly from a drawing by Homer, who may, indeed, have done the drawing on the stone as well. The print, entitled "Jamaica Pond West Roxbury, Mass. 1858," is very uncommon though we have handled three or four impressions of it in the last forty years. One of these we sold in 1941 to the late Raymond S. Wilkins, later Chief Justice of Massachusetts, but then a practicing attorney and counsel for the Donnelly Advertising Company. It was a wedding present to the daughter of James M. Curley, who was being married to a Donnelly son. The gift was especially appropriate, for the Curley mansion overlooked the scene pictured in the lithograph.

A few years later after Mrs. Donnelly's premature death, I mentioned the print to Albert West, a lawyer who had been made chairman of the Recreation Commission of the City of Boston. West had considerable imagination for a politician and had been decorating the Commission's office with appropriate prints. I remembered particularly the lithograph of Boston boys coasting on the Common. I suggested that he might be able to persuade Curley to part with the skating scene. He succeeded and the print hung for a time in the office of the City Hall Annex. Some years later as West's connection with the city government was being terminated he asked me to make an offer to buy the print, but nothing came of it and through some arrangement or other it passed once more into the Chief Justice's possession. From him it passed by inheritance to his widow.

Another fine and colorful skating scene, after a drawing by Homer and lithographed by Bufford, "Skating on Central Park, New York," appeared in 1861. Like the Jamaica Pond print it is rare. We were fortunate in being able to buy a fine impression a year ago and to place it in the hands of a Homer collector. In the meantime the demand for Homer's woodcuts continues unabated. Indeed, the value of these prints has risen to the point where thieves have begun to make a practice of cutting them out of files of periodicals in public collections.

* * * * * * * * *

110

WITH FREEDOM TO THINK

THOMAS CLAP (1703-1767) was graduated from Harvard College in 1722 but for the last twenty-two years of his life he presided over the younger and more conservative collegiate institution in New Haven as "one of the three men who were chiefly responsible for shaping one of the great universities of the world. How much of what he did was for good and how much for ill, who are we to judge?" (Shipton, *Sibley's Harvard Graduates*.)

Yale having been founded partly as a reaction to the liberalism already creeping into its sister college, it fell to President Clap to maintain its orthodox position.

"To this end" writes Shipton, "he departed from the old Harvard policy of permitting and even aiding the innoculation of the students with heretical theology in order to build up an immunity for their later years. When some of the Yale seniors had taken up a subscription for reprinting Locke's *Essay on Toleration*, he called them in and demanded that they, on penalty of losing their degrees, make a public confession of their sin in so doing. One boy refused and found his name left out of the catalogue on Commencement Day. He finally obtained his degree by threatening to appeal to the King in Council."

The edition of Locke's *Essay* published at the instigation of the Yale seniors was printed in Boston by Rogers and Fowle in 1743. Copies of it may be found in a number of institutions, but I recall having had but one, thirty-five years ago. It was given by the future founder of Dartmouth College to a colleague and contained an

111

inscription "For the Rev. and Mrs. Hez. Bissell Pastor of Wintonbury. From his Friend & Brother E. Wheelock, Lebanon Jan:17, AD 1743,4." It was bought by the Dartmouth College Library from funds supplied by the McGregor College Plan.

Locke's writings had an essential role in the development of American political thought in the eighteenth century, and the *Essays on Toleration*, intolerable in New Haven in 1743, were so highly valued by Thomas Hollis "the republican" a generation later that he had published at his own expense an elaborate edition of which a copy was sent to the Harvard College Library. Hollis's edition was bound in red morocco, with the Liberty-cap on the spine panels, the figure of an owl in gilt on the front cover and on the back the words "Ense petit Placidam sub Libertate Quietem" a quotation from Algernon Sidney which was later incorporated as a motto in the seal of the Commonwealth.

There is in my own library a copy of Hollis's edition in its symbolically decorated red morocco, which is my excuse for introducing it in these pages. The spirit of freedom that has prevailed at Harvard from the seventeenth to the twentieth century is, I like to think, exemplified by a letter which stands on the shelf alongside the Locke.

In 1916, when the first World War was in its earliest days, and sentiment in New England was strong for intervention on the side of the western allies, there taught at Harvard a great psychologist by the name of Hugo Munsterberg. He was a German national and made no secret about his loyalty to the fatherland. The United States being at that time in a state of strict neutrality, he was entirely within his rights, but feelings ran hot, and there were demands from alumni committed to the allied cause that he be expelled from the Harvard faculty.

One of these alumni, Alfred C. Lane of the class of 1883, and a professor at Tufts University so expressed himself to President Lowell who replied in this masterly letter:

112

The Corporation has considered carefully the case of Munsterberg, and has found no proof of any conduct relating to the present war that would justify his dismissal from the service of the University.

Everyone would, I presume, agree that no language or conduct in regard to any one of the belligerent nations would justify removal, unless it would compel the same action if used in connection with any other of those nations.

It has fallen to the lot of this University to be among the foremost in maintaining the principle of academic freedom, which has been severely strained by the present war. That principle, we believe to be of the greatest importance, and not to be put in jeopardy without tangible proof of personal misconduct, apart from the unpopularity of the views expressed.

The phrase which I have picked for the title of this chapter is taken, of course, from the final stanza of the Ode by the Reverend Samuel Gilman of Charleston, South Carolina composed for the Centennial Celebration of Harvard University in 1836. The Ode sometimes known as *Fair Harvard*, was first printed in the order of service for that occasion. Despite the dreadful second and third stanzas, the words of this hymn have had a deep emotional appeal on Harvard men and women for nearly a century and a half.

My copy of the broadside on which they were first printed was used by the author's wife as writing paper, on which she wrote a friend in Charleston:

I send you a copy of Mr. Gilman's Ode as I know your interest in everything connected with your pastor. It excited great enthusiasm among the Alumni whose tender recollections were awakened by the occasion. Mrs. Quincey said to me, when we were dining there yesterday — 'it seems as if Mr. Gilman had been *sent here* to write that Ode!' . . .

* * * * * * * * *

113

BOSTON COLLECTORS*

ON THE WHOLE women have not been conspicuous in the ranks of collectors, but their contribution to the tradition of bibliophily has been great, and I propose to begin this chapter with an account of two Boston ladies whose collections were of major importance.

The first of these is Susan Minns, whose collection of books, manuscripts and prints illustrating *The Dance of Death* was sold by auction at the American Art Association in 1922, with which year we begin our half century of bibliophiles. This remarkable woman, who was twenty-one years old at the outbreak of the Civil War and died on the eve of World War II, began her collection when as a child she was given books illustrated with woodcuts by illustrators of the time.

"I was shown," she wrote later, "how woodcuts were printed and even tried my hand at making [wood] blocks. So that quite early I began to buy anything that had a woodcut. When I came upon Holbein, I also found Dürer, the *Livres d'Heures*, and horae, and very many prints, most enchanting."

She joined a class at the Museum of Fine Arts, where under the encouragement of S.R. Koehler she became a serious collector of the illustrations of *The Dance of Death*, a favorite theme of printers and illustrators from the fifteenth and sixteenth centuries. The auction catalogue of her collection listed sixty printed books of hours of this

---

* This chapter is the text of a talk entitled "A Half-Century of Boston Bibliophiles" given by George Goodspeed at a meeting of the Bostonian Society on 27 April 1982.

period and a score of manuscripts from the thirteenth to the sixteenth centuries. The books in these categories alone would today bring many times the $24,000 realized by the entire collection of 1000 lots in 1922.

A native of the town of Lincoln, Miss Minns lived for most of her life at Number 14 Louisburg Square. She was a true-born collector, pursuing her subject with imagination and determination. The extent of the latter characteristic in her personality is well illustrated in a story about the Minns dog and the Boston Athenaeum. On one occasion when Miss Minns brought her beloved pet with her to 10½ Beacon Street she was told that dogs were not allowed on the premises. Remarking "We'll see about that" she marched down Beacon Hill to her broker's office, bought a share in the Athenaeum, registered it in the dog's name, returned to the library, slapped the share certificate on the front desk, and said "*Now* keep him out!"

Miss Minns was a charter member of the Marine Biological Institute at Woods Hole, a generous benefactor of Wellesley College and the Massachusetts Institute of Technology, of which latter institution she was the oldest alumna. She was a botanical scholar and a contributor to Gray's *Manual of Botany*. Among her other philanthropies was the gift of Little Wachusett Mountain to the Commonwealth of Massachusetts for a bird sanctuary. She died in her ninety-ninth year, having survived the sale of her collection by sixteen years.

Amy Lowell was the other of our two lady bibliophiles. It was in the huge book-walled room of her house that for the first time I was exposed to the riches of a great private library. I was brought there by my father in the autumn of 1925 ostensibly to be his amanuensis while he prepared the appraisal of Miss Lowell's library for estate purposes. I say ostensibly, for I suspect the real purpose of my minor participation was intended to be educational.

Miss Lowell's first acquisition was a copy of *Rollo Learning to Read* which she wheedled out of an indulgent mother at a very early age. The book "aroused such a covetous desire in my small mind," she afterwards wrote, "as to shake it to its foundations." At sixteen she made the acquaintance of the famous bookseller Bernard Quaritch then visiting in Boston and by 1898 she was buying original books of William Blake in Quaritch's London shop.

At the time of her premature death in 1925, she had built a library of 12,000 volumes. Particularly rich in first editions and manuscripts of the Romantic Period, it became one of the cornerstones of the Houghton Library collection.

State Street was in those days well populated with scholar-collectors. Among them the name of Harold Murdock comes first to mind. After twenty years in banking, he retired in 1920 to assume the directorship of the Harvard University Press. The perfect image of an eighteenth century gentleman, Murdock was wont to remark, as a matter of course, that had he lived in eighteenth century Boston, he would have been a Tory, as would any gentleman. Though, indeed, when it came to England in the earlier part of the century he tended to be a Jacobite, reflecting his Scottish ancestry. He had a small choice library of Johnsoniana as well as rare pamphlets, prints and broadsides relating to the American Revolution. His taste ran to books in fine bindings, old or even new, preferring such to shabby copies in their original state. An historian as well as bibliophile, Murdock was the author of several monographs in the writing of which he made good use of original materials — books, maps, engravings and manuscripts, in his collection. In his account of the battles of Concord and Lexington, for example, he reproduced contemporary views of the engagements as evidence of what really happened on that historic day. Like his companion volume on Bunker Hill, and, indeed, all of his writing, it is very readable. His *1872, Letters Describing the Great Boston Fire*, though written as fiction is the most accurate and well-documented history of that unhappy event which we have. A fictional conversation in Revolutionary Boston, entitled *Earl Percy's Dinner Table*, gives a colorful picture of our town in those troubled times.

Two of his books, *The Life of Sir William Kirkaldy of Grange*,

Knight and *Notes on a Country Library*, were privately printed for the Club of Odd Volumes by D.B. Updike and Bruce Rogers, respectively.

I venture to mention these writings of Murdock because they are little known today and will repay the attention of any reader who has an antiquarian turn of mind.

Mr. and Mrs. Percival Merritt, who lived on Marlborough Street, were friends of Murdock and shared his preoccupation with the eighteenth century. Sidney Smith engraved two bookplates for the Merritts. One of them, based on Spitzweg's picture of "The Bookworm" is enlivened by the addition of the Merritt family kittens, adding a playful touch to the familiar picture. The other bookplate, used on their Horace Walpole collection, featured a portrait of H.W. with a view of Strawberry Hill below it. The Walpole collection was the most complete one in this country at the time, and was given to Harvard by Mrs. Merritt after her husband's death in 1932.

Merritt was also a collector of little juveniles published by the Newbery family of London in the late eighteenth century and for these he had D.B. Updike supply an appropriate little label using an original woodcut by Bewick. These Lilliputian books with such engaging titles as *The Renowned History of Giles Gingerbread* and *Nurse Trulove's Christmas-Box* have always been popular with collectors and the Merritt collection was a very large one.

Merritt, like Murdock, issued a number of privately printed books based on his own collection. Two small volumes, *Horace Walpole, Printer* and *An Account of Descriptive Catalogues of Strawberry Hill*, were printed by Bruce Rogers in 1907 and 1915 in editions of 77 and 75 copies each. Rogers was also the printer of *Piozzi Marginalia* edited by Merritt and published by the Harvard University Press in 1925. In the same year, he also wrote an amusing little parody entitled *The History of Little Billy & His Grand-Pa*, which featured Professor George Lyman Kittredge as "Grand-Pa" and was printed in the style of the Newbery toy books. Two copies of it were printed at the Merrymount Press, but in anticipation of a wider demand, a second impression of eleven copies was run off immediately afterwards.

A Chestnut Hill neighbor of Murdock's was Daniel E. Kennedy, whose lanky frame was a familiar sight in the many book shops then surviving in Boston. There must have been seasons when he appeared without them, but in my recollection he is always associated with a long topcoat and an umbrella, which latter implement seemed ready to poke through files of second-hand books that might come its way. A felt hat sat squarely atop an aquiline face whence protruded a long cigar held firmly between the front teeth. He had a sardonic sense of humor and was secretive about his extensive collection which, indeed, he never exposed to visitors. One of his principal interests was the American novelist Charles Brockden Brown in whose bibliography and biography he felt that he had a proprietary interest.

Being of independent means, Kennedy had the time to spend going the rounds of the booksellers and possessed the rare instinct of knowing where a new private library was being picked over by the bookseller who had just bought it. He had an uncanny knack of pulling the best book from an unprocessed pile and pressing the startled owner to price it then and there. Naturally, he usually got a bargain. He was what we call today a loner, and he had few, if any, friends among other collectors. He was quick to sense what he thought to be a slight, and left in his will a provision that under no circumstances was one particular dealer, from whom he had bought much of his collection, to be permitted to participate in its dispersal.

Frank Brewer Bemis, sportsman and financier, was the most important Boston bibliophile of this century. He retired from the senior partnership of Estabrook and Company in 1923, thereafter devoting most of his time to the pursuit of salmon, birds and books. Amicably separated from his wife, he lived the life of a wealthy bachelor with ample time and means to devote to his hobbies. His interest in books went back to the early years of this century and continued unabated until his death in 1935.

His appearance was all that might be expected of a man in his position: thick set, florid complexion, close cropped hair, well clipped moustache, pince nez, derby hat, short gabardine topcoat. Though naturally shy, he had numerous friends, especially in the many Boston and New York clubs of which he was a member. As befitted that of a proper Bostonian, his great book collection was not widely known, so that when the city assessors of Beverly valued the contents of his house, they ignored the library entirely. When Mr. Bemis called attention to the omission, the official commented "Oh books. Not worth much are they? Shall we say a quarter a piece?" Bemis allowed as how he thought them worth a bit more than that, and the unit value was accordingly raised to half a dollar.

Bemis's was undoubtedly the most valuable collection of literature ever made in Boston, ranging in time from Caxton in the fifteenth century to Edwin Arlington Robinson in the twentieth.

As early as 1924, Bemis gave his collection to Harold Murdock and another friend, John Woodbury, as trustees for the Children's Hospital, retaining physical possession of the library with the right to improve it by addition or exchange as opportunity might arise. After the donor's death, the trustees were to sell the books for the benefit of the hospital, the method of disposal being left to their discretion.

Bemis lived for eleven years after the gift, and added greatly to the collection during that time. Murdock predeceased him and was replaced as trustee by Francis Hart of the Old Colony Trust Company and United Fruit. Hart himself was a collector of books on the West Indies and the author of *Admirals of the Caribbean* published in 1922 and recently reprinted.

After Bemis's death, the trustees consigned his collection to the Rosenbach Company of New York by whom it was sold off gradually over the next nine years, with the substantial remnant remaining at that time sold *en bloc* to a Boston bookseller. The details of the liquidation, from which the original consignee profited handsomely have been recounted elsewhere and need not be repeated here.

Both the Bemis and Lowell collections contained many fine

books and manuscripts of John Keats, which, with the collection of Fred Holland Day are the subject of a little volume entitled *Keats and the Bostonians.*

Day is better remembered as a pioneer in fine art photography and as the active partner in the short-lived publishing house of Copeland and Day. He was a recluse, bedridden by his own choice for the last sixteen years of his life. His Keats collection, with additions from that of Mr. Bemis and others, was exhibited at the Boston Public Library in 1921, but the famous letters from Keats's fiancée to his sister were jealously guarded by Day until his death.

The name of William A. Sargent is not much remembered today, nor indeed was it widely known in his own, but his library was such an important one that he is entitled to more than a casual reference. Sargent was a Bostonian by birth, prepared for college at Roxbury Latin, graduated from Amherst College in 1872 and Boston University Law School two years later. He practiced law for twenty-five years after which he retired to devote his attention to his investments. He was so successful in this occupation that his services came to be in demand as an adviser to trustees and other fiduciaries. The fees which he collected from these clients helped to finance his book buying, and bills which he rendered were often made out in odd amounts of dollars and cents, conforming to the latest bills from his booksellers.

Sargent's collection consisted primarily of French illustrated books from the fifteenth to the nineteenth centuries, though its heaviest concentration was in the eighteenth. Shortly before his death, he became concerned about the risk of fire in the old Brookline apartment house where he had lived for many years, and deposited his choicest treasures in the Museum of Fine Arts where he visited them faithfully twice a week. They, with the rest of his collection, eventually went to the museum by bequest.

With his bejowled countenance usually ornamented by the remains of a half-smoked cigar whose ashes were not always brushed off the waistcoat below, he was not altogether prepossessing in appearance. Henry Rossiter, of the museum, wrote that "suavities of speech and dress, to which in his own life he was frankly indifferent failed to beguile him." It is not surprising then that, though a member of bookish groups, he made few friends among them. But his taste in books was impeccable.

Equally impeccable in his taste for books, but at the opposite end of the sartorial scale was William K. Richardson, known in his Oxford days as the "Duke of Balliol."

A few years younger than Sargent, Richardson was always beautifully turned out. His well groomed walrus moustache practically bristled with importance. In a superbly tailored dinner jacket with pearl-studded shirt front, he was a truly imposing figure. In short, a swell, perhaps the ultimate survivor of a vanished species.

He was, like Sargent, a bachelor and a lawyer. A graduate of Harvard College *summa cum laude* in the classics, he entered Balliol after graduation and took his B.A. at Oxford in 1884. Returning to Boston, he joined the law firm later known as Fish, Richardson and Neave, and currently, following the fashion of our own time, as Fish and Richardson.

During the last decade of his life, Richardson's collecting was actively encouraged by William A. Jackson of the Houghton Library, so that Dr. William Bond of that institution was able to describe the Richardson bequest as "one of the most magnificent . . . that have come to the library," where it may be seen today in a special room designed to the testator's order.

The attentive at this point may have noted that there has been no mention of any collectors of what is loosely referred to as Americana: books relating to the early history of our country and specifically of our region, such as made up the "New England Library" of Thomas Prince, Boston's first bibliophile. The fact is that since the passing of the first generation of the Hollingsworth family around the turn of this century, we had no local collectors of books of the early colonial period until Matt Jones came along.

Jones was a native Vermonter who came to Boston by way of

Dartmouth and Harvard Law School. He proceeded from the practice of law to the presidency of the New England Telephone and Telegraph Company, from which he retired in 1936.

Though he bought Vermontiana in a small way as early as 1905, most of his buying was done in the late 'twenties and early 'thirties. He was another of our scholar-collectors, for whom rarity was in itself a matter of no consequence. He had no use for what bookmen contemptuously describe as "postage stamps," and there were few such among the two thousand or so items in his collection which covered the period from the settlement of Boston to the end of the Revolution.

Jones left behind him a catalogue of the collection, painstakingly written out in neat longhand on 5" x 8" cards, with collations, descriptions of each book, the year of acquisition, price and name of bookseller from whom purchased, and other pertinent information.

More limited in size and scope was the collection of early travellers to the far West by Donald McKay Frost, a transplanted South Carolinian.

He was wealthy in his own right and by marriage, and he looked it. Too well dressed for a Bostonian, though he lived here for almost fifty years, he was an unreconstructed southerner to the end, remarking on one occasion that he was not an admirer of Lincoln.

Frost had begun collecting in his undergraduate days, with modern English first editions. Eventually Oscar Wilde and G.B. Shaw lost their appeal and he became interested in the discovery and development of the Rocky Mountain region. His collection of Western Americana included many of the rare guide books of the gold rush era and was given some time before his death to the American Antiquarian Society of which he was a member.

Many of you, I am sure, will remember Albert Whittier, the "Brother" of "C.W. Whittier & Bro." He had a fine collection of American engravings and early American furniture, some English sporting books, a good run of Dickens first editions in the original parts, and a fairly extensive collection of Rudyard Kipling.

One of Whittier's good friends was Roger Amory who was making a collection of books and materials relating to the history of the book. Knowing of this interest, Whittier, as a gift for his friend, got together a little lot of pre-Gutenberg specimens of book-making, including a clay cone of the third century B.C., a Chinese wood block of the eleventh century, some specimens of papyrus, and the like.

Amory was a professional Boston trustee who used to finance his book buying with his corporate director's fees. As he held eighteen of these directorships in 1933, his buying was not too greatly constrained thereby. Though his library was not great in bulk, it included a leaf from the *Gutenberg Bible*, some English translations of the classics, some fine illuminated manuscripts and a remarkable lot of Darwin first editions and manuscripts.

About 1950, Amory resigned from his various directorships, withdrew his name from *Who's Who*, and retired to Boca Grande, Florida. There he built a handsome library building for that resort community which he named for Gutenberg's partner, Johannes Fust, and deposited his collection in it. He organized a program of supplying books for the outlying islands, believing that, as he said, if one boy from these primitive settlements was inspired by access to reading, all of his efforts would be repaid. During the last ten years of his life he endured the pains of terminal cancer. He once wrote "I have a higher regard for mankind than man, and a higher regard for woman than womankind."

A neighbor of Albert Whittier, some fifteen years his junior, was Carleton Richmond, who died seven years ago in his ninetieth year. A quiet, self-effacing man, conservative in dress, manner and politics, he built from small beginnings what he referred to as a "modest library, specializing in flower books and herbals." In addition to the horticultural books, there were some fine literary first editions from the Bemis and Murdock collections, and a really important collection of the diarists Pepys and Evelyn which he gave to the Houghton when he was still active.

The most exciting piece in the Richmond collection was a manuscript herbal which Kraus, the New York bookseller, offered in 1951 for $16,000. Last fall, after an interval of thirty years, it was sold at auction by Richmond's heirs for $225,000, a substantial advance, one must agree, even taking inflation and interest charges into account.

Richmond's generosity to the Houghton Library was not limited to gifts of books from his own collection. When money was needed for some special purchase, he was one of the Friends to whom Jackson of the Houghton first turned for help. Thus, in 1947 when our firm had acquired the New York Public Library duplicate of the original broadside printing of the *Declaration of Independence*, it was Richmond who came up with the $4,000 asked. Jackson was criticized by President Conant for spending so much money on a piece of paper, but a copy has since sold for more than a hundred times that much.

It seems remarkable that but one of our Boston bibliophiles devoted himself to collecting the fruits of the flowering of New England, the golden age of Bryant, Emerson, Longfellow, Thoreau, Holmes, Hawthorne, Lowell and Whittier. There have been other great collections made of the works of those classic writers, but they were made by outlanders.

Parkman D. Howe was born in Brookline in 1889 and began collecting books seriously in 1931, with first editions of John Greenleaf Whittier, who was a schoolmate of Mr. Howe's grandfather a century earlier at the Haverhill Academy. The scope of the collection was soon widened to include not only the authors I have mentioned but New England writers of all periods, from the seventeenth century on down, so that the number of authors represented ran to twenty or more, with a number of great books from the earlier period. Among these early writers is Anne Bradstreet whose *Poems* first appeared in London in 1650 and in Boston in 1678. Both editions are rare, especially that printed in Boston. Mrs. Bradstreet's were the first secular poems known to be written in this country, and they represent the first literary effort of any American woman.

The Howe collection, now at the University of Florida at Gainesville, will, however, always be best known for the wealth of its nineteenth century collections and for the many association volumes which it contains. Howe was an aggressive collector and didn't give up easily when on the track of an elusive rarity. On one occasion he pursued a little Whittier pamphlet from Nantucket to Manhattan and Atlanta before running it to earth in Seattle. The Whittier section of the Howe catalogue runs to more than eighty pages and contains practically all of the rarities of that author as well as important manuscripts. He had those two great desiderata of collectors: *Justice and Expediency* and *Moll Pitcher*, both inscribed by the author.

Mr. Howe's Emerson collection was in a way the most impressive in his library. Of particular interest are two relics of Emerson's Boston days: the two printings of his *Letter to the Second Church and Society.* This historic document marked Emerson's break with organized religion, and Mr. Howe was able to collar not only one of the six known pamphlet printings of it but one of the three recorded copies of the broadside printing on satin.

It is sad, in a way, to see such bibliographical riches leave here for the deep South, but one must remember that Emerson himself was a missionary to Florida many years ago — he preached sermons in Key West when he was twenty-three years old!

With the coming of Frederick Meek to Boston in 1946, the pulpit of the Old South Church was occupied by a book collector for the first time since Thomas Prince died in 1758. Dr. Meek was a native of Audley in Staffordshire, and grew up on Cape Breton Island. He brought to the Old South great natural talents — a fine speaking voice, commanding presence in the pulpit, a delightful sense of humor and an affectionate nature, and consequently enjoyed the esteem and affection not only of his parishoners but of the whole community. He had become a collector, in a small way, of the poet Whittier when, in the winter of 1954-55, he fell victim to a throat condition which precluded all use of his voice for the better part of a year. During this time, usually accompanied by Mrs. Meek to do the talking, he spent many days going the round of the Boston book shops with his want list, filling the gaps in his collection. And after these protracted months of enforced silence, he continued to devote much of his leisure to pursuing his hobby.

Inevitably the Whittier collection reached a degree of completion where he had to look further afield, and he became involved with Holmes and some of the other New England writers. He was very popular with booksellers, who tended to favor him above other customers when a desirable bit came along. Occasionally, when encountering something he particularly coveted but which was beyond his means, he would say (especially just before Christmas) "Why don't you offer this to Mrs. Meek?" Needless to say, his wife was delighted to have her Christmas gift problems solved so easily. During the year or so before his death, Dr. Meek had begun negotiating with Whittier College in California for the sale of his Whittier books, manuscripts and memorabilia *en bloc*, a sale consumated a year later.

Having travelled the half century from Minns to Meek, I am keenly aware that this coverage of the period is sorely inadequate. Nothing has been said about the great medical collection of Harvey Cushing, of Augustin Parker's *Vicars*, Rosamund Loring's marbled papers, C.E. Goodspeed's Ruskins, Carl Keller's *Don Quixotes*, Stephen W. Phillips's voyages, Chief Justice Wilkins's Civil War books or Lee Friedman's Judaica. Nor have I mentioned George A. Plimpton of Ginn and Company, benefactor of Exeter, Amherst and Wellesley, whose collection of school books is now at Columbia. His imposing figure, appearing on the threshold of a book shop had all the aura of an impending visit from royalty.

Dr. Timothy Leary (no relation), Harvey Cushing's medical school classmate and Medical Examiner for half of Boston, connoisseur of maps and authority on the life of Dr. Benjamin Church managed to squeeze in visits to the shops between post mortems. He might have bumped into Walter Lewisson, a greybearded salesman from Shreve, Crump and Low, looking for books with George

Washington's name on the title-page. In his bachellor apartment at the Vendome, Lewisson stored thousands of bits and pieces of Washingtoniana, each carefully entered in a thick pocket notebook which was always with him. When he sold the collection to the Huntington Library for a whopping $10,000, the book world was amazed. A magpie of equal industry was J. Francis Driscoll, organist at the Cathedral of the Holy Cross, whose Brookline garage was stuffed with a quarter of a million pieces of sheet music. When the senior J.K. Lilly bought all of Driscoll's Stephen Foster songs for his Foster Hall collection and the younger Lilly bought the Jerome Kerns for the Library of Congress, the bulk was not perceptibly diminished.

The library of St. Lawrence University in Canton, New York, is richer for the fine Hawthorne collection given to it by Ulysses S. Milburn, the hearty Universalist parson of Melrose, as is Boston College for the Francis Thompson collection which owes its genesis to the gentle Jesuit, Terence Connolly.

To say nothing of the myriad small collectors who used to spend their lunch hours browsing in the shops: Alexander Towns and his Lafcadio Hearns; Max Weinberg, a lesser bureaucrat in the State House, and his Hemingways; Rowland Patrick, partner in W.K. Richardson's old law firm; Beatrice Gunn, the dowdy little spinster with a passion for children's books; Felix Matton, who used to vend newspapers and cigarettes at the Armstrong Transfer kiosk in the South Station; nor that eccentric collector of fine sets whose library of thousands of volumes — each one carefully wrapped in newspaper and kept in cartons in the attic of an old North Shore mansion, to be gloated over by their solitary owner like a miser and his gold — that vast attic eventually reduced to rubble in a catastrophic fire from which its owner walked away to disappear from the world of books forever. Well, they are all gone, and so is my time, and I fear, your patience. Thank you!

* * * * * * * * *

At Nº2 Milk St. Old South Branch
GOODSPEED'S BOOK SHOP
A NATIONAL INSTITUTION
Dealing in Old & Modern Books, Autographs
& Prints of all kinds
STRANGERS ESPECIALLY INVITED
When in Boston Browse in Goodspeed's

By permission of the Houghton Library, Harvard University
Original sign for the "Old South Branch"

Appendices

Appendix A *

HOW GOODSPEED'S BEGAN

I am asked to preface this catalogue with some account of the early days of Goodspeed's. The part is not wholly to my liking. There is something terrifying in the "dark backward and abysm of time." In these troubled times I feel with Dante:

> *Like one cast breathless, gasping, from the spray,*
> *Who eyes the watery perils from the shore.*

It would be far pleasanter for me to think of miraculous putts on Southern greens keeping my score below ninety, the ecstatic thrill of a well-placed fly over the rising trout, or the unfolding blooms next June of Japanese iris. Dreams, dreams—the sobering hand of Time on the shoulder begins to be felt as one approaches seventy.

But we do not want your moralizing, the staff tells me. Give us some reminiscences, please. And so, trivial as they may seem, I will jot down some recollections which the re-examination of two hundred and forty-nine predecessors to the present catalogue brings to mind. Catalogue No. 1 appeared in October of 1899, toward the close of my first year's experience as a bookseller. I well remember the gratitude which I felt on reading Ernest Dressel North's generous comment on it in *The Book Buyer*, "a very creditable effort for a first catalogue" (quoting from memory). Considering that my book knowledge had been acquired in the casual encounters of a limited purse in the secondhand shops and auction rooms, Mr. North's commendation was perhaps justified. As I look back and painfully recall the few dollars which made up my capital at the start, I marvel that

---

* Foreword to Goodspeed's Catalogue 250, by Charles Eliot Goodspeed (1935).

the business survived those early days and could make its bow to the army of catalogue readers with a collection of some variety and interest. I notice one word on the cover which I should now in candor correct. The catalogue was hardly a "selection"—it was rather a list of the whole stock at the time! Occasionally my lack of literary knowledge and training betrayed itself in some lamentable error. For example, one day the learned and eccentric son of Edward Everett, Dr. William Everett, was in the store and when mention was made of the fads of collecting he exclaimed, "My hobby is collecting errors, for example" (here he darted at a copy of this first catalogue and, opening it at random, he shouted), "'Thackery' has two *'a's'*!" The present catalogue has one thing in common with that first effort, in that while it of course cannot pretend to such completeness of representation of the stock as did the first list with 718 titles, it does represent practically a cross section of our entire stock in nearly every department, and in this respect it is also typical of many of its predecessors.

Although this is not intended as an autobiographical sketch, I may perhaps be expected to say a word about my introduction to the occupation of bookselling. To those older readers who recall the depression of 1893 and the years immediately following it is quite unnecessary to explain how I found myself in the fall of 1898 without a job. The silver lining in that cloud was the opportunity of fulfilling a long cherished desire. Now, I said, I can do what I always wished to do, I can try bookselling. For I loved books—old books and everything associated with them. The past three years of my previous employment in quite a different line of merchandise had been spent in lower New York, and naturally Ann Street was a convenient and seductive noontime resort. So when the question of a change was forced upon me I went to Isaac Mendoza, who still occupies the store at No. 15 which I haunted in those early days, and said to him, "Mr. Mendoza, I have lost my job in New York. I am going back to Boston and in these times there are no new jobs to get. I am thinking of going into the secondhand book business. What do you think of my chances?" I got my first encouragement from his reply, "I never knew but one man who failed in it and that was Tom _____, and he played the races." With this slight encouragement, I then invested the few hundred dollars I had saved in miscellaneous purchases at Bangs' Auction Room and some "remainders" from Mendoza, including a lot of books from the bankrupt stock of Stone & Kimball, of which Mendoza had been a large buyer. Coming to Boston I called at Libbie's Auction Room. "Mr. Libbie," I said, "You have known me for a number of years" (as a buyer of little things with small profit to him, I fear!) "and I am thinking of opening a secondhand book store. What do you think of my prospects?" "Mr. Goodspeed," he replied, "if you can get a job at $20 a week, don't think of going into the secondhand book business." I was leaving a salary of $2,700 a year paid by the agricultural implement company for which I had worked for fifteen years. (How vividly I recall the winter months, travelling over Prince Edward Island, Nova Scotia, New Brunswick, Aroostook County, Maine, etc.; the long winter drives over beautiful roads bordered by snow-laden spruce or hemlock, solitary but delightful.) And $20 a week seemed a meager sum on which to support a family. But the die was cast. Like others in similar cases I was not looking for advice, I wanted encouragement. Although Mr. Libbie failed me in that, he was nevertheless very helpful and a good friend during the whole period of our relationship, which terminated with his death in 1904.

Back in Boston with my few boxes of books I had next to find a store or "shop" as I called it. (Most book dealers had "Book Stores" in those days. "Book Shop" seemed a little nicer to me, and so I adopted the word.) The most direct way of getting a store, I thought, was to go to a real estate office, and I chanced into Whittier's Agency, where I was politely received. The first question asked was how much rent I wished to pay for the small premises I was looking for, the clerk at the same time pulling out the drawer of his card index. I replied, "Not over $50 a month." Bang closed the drawer! Driven to become my own agent I wandered around in a district which seemed promising. I had fixed upon the vicinity of Boston Common as being desirable. Walking up Park Street, I saw, about half way up to Beacon Street, a basement window with the sign "To Let." The rent, $55, I thought I could manage. Christmas was at hand. The beautifully printed books of Stone & Kimball (for the most part not greatly distinguished in contents, but attractively bound) at twenty-five cents were offered as a suggestion of something between a Christmas card and a gift, and I found that the ladies of Beacon Hill and the Back Bay were very appreciative of the opportunity of getting an acceptable gift-remembrance for so slight a sum. The odd volumes of the Stone & Kimball edition of Poe at fifty cents were very popular, and my own private collection of Ruskin and Dr. Thomas William Parsons, the translator of Dante, whose verse had appealed to me and whose books I had collected, gave a slightly superior flavor to the stock. For furniture, I had a chair and also a wooden box, covered with denim and stood on end, which made a sufficient desk. A shelf, nailed inside the box and holding three volumes of *American Book Prices Current* (all that were published at the time), comprised my reference library. My first day's receipts were something over $20. (In those days of wisdom, before the government claimed a partnership in the business, I reckoned no transaction in my sales until the books had been paid for.)

The game was now on. Of course I wanted to have a slogan, and after much laborious thought, I adopted the motto "Anything that's a book," the meaning of this being that I intended to try to have something to interest all classes of buyers. The little phrase has been a source of embarrassment at times, however, being quoted against me by disappointed would-be sellers when I have turned down their offers of books which I could not use. A motto should have a trademark to bear it. The Heintzemann Press happily suggested the bookish idea of a tonsured monk absorbed in the reading of his homily as he rode. The facsimile given on the following page is from the first rough draft before the motto evolved into its final form.

Of course the great difficulty with a new bookseller who has little money is to find stock to replenish his shelves. What money I

could get I could not afford to put out in a few rare items. I had to have quantity. Even then I found difficulty in getting enough books, so I was for a while driven to the device of constant rearranging of the stock. Monday morning ·the rear shelves would be moved to the front, the top shelves to the middle, the middle to the bottom, and so on, so that even the most frequent visitor often remarked on the rapidity with which the stock was replenished.

My relations with other booksellers were from the start, as they always have been, most cordial. Prominent among the dealers in the early days was that dean of the Boston secondhand book trade, George Emery Littlefield of 67 Cornhill. Mr. Littlefield was a Harvard graduate and had a decided bent toward historical study. He specialized in Americana, particularly in genealogies. I found in Littlefield a good friend, always most helpful, and in return I made no effort to enter the field of genealogical books, in which there seemed to be hardly enough profit to support more than one dealer. This reminds me of a story told by my good friend and neighbor, Andrew McCance, when introducing me to a customer the other day. "You see," he said, "Mr. Goodspeed and I have an understanding between us by which he sends people having Christian Science literature to sell to me, and I turn over the Americana to him. Like Tony, who had a sidewalk permit for his fruit stand from the Bank. A friend asked him for a loan of ten dollars. Tony was sorry but, 'I have agree' with da Bank. They no let me.' 'What you meana, they no let you?' 'Well, when I come here, they say, "Tony, we no sell da banan, you no loana da mon."'" Littlefield was brusque in manner and not tolerant of casual visitors. When I was in his store one day a woman called with a bundle of books to sell—trash of course. "Don't want them," was the curt comment. The owner was persistent—"What's the matter with them?" "They are not old enough." "Not old enough?

Here's one printed almost a hundred years ago." "I want books more than a hundred years old." Exit, with the indignant retort, "Huh! They didn't print books that old."

George D. Morse of Haverhill was Mr. Libbie's auctioneer and one of the keenest and most prominent auctioneers whom I have ever known, although I think the late Stan V. Henkels of Philadelphia was almost as good in this line. One day Morse invited himself to lunch with me, and in return offered some helpful suggestions in regard to the book business. One of these I remember with amusement. "When you get out your Americana catalogue," he said (he had offered me the use of his own mailing list), "be sure and put in a set of *The New England Historic Genealogical Register.*" "But I haven't a set," I replied innocently. "Makes no difference," he answered, "Littlefield always has one, and if you get an order he will have to give you a dealer's commission." Mr. Libbie, also, generously placed at my service his own mailing list for my first catalogue, as was his practice with all young booksellers.

I do not find in either Catalogue No. 1 or the one which followed it five months later any item of particular interest to-day. When we come to Catalogue No. 3, however, there are some Thoreau first editions which are perhaps worthy of mention. This catalogue offered two copies of *A Week on the Concord and Merrimack Rivers* and *Walden.* One copy of the *Week* was in a slightly damaged binding, but included five lines in pencil by Thoreau on page 396. That copy was priced at $15. One copy of *Walden*, described as in spotless condition, was offered for $12. The other copy of the *Week* was a presentation from Thoreau to his sister, with suitable inscription in Thoreau's autograph, and the other *Walden* was Thoreau's own, with his autograph on the flyleaf and occasional pencilled memoranda by him throughout the book. Someone got these two books for $75, which was a bargain even in those days when American first editions could be had for prices which look very low now. I presume that these Thoreaus were brought to me by Frank B. Sanborn, then the relic of the famous Concord literary group.

Sanborn was at one time a tutor in Emerson's family and was, of course, acquainted with Thoreau. These books probably came to him either from Miss Sophia Thoreau's estate, or from Thoreau's friend, William Ellery Channing (not the Unitarian preacher of that name, but the Concord recluse and poet who wrote *Thoreau the Poet Naturalist*).

Sanborn was a frequent visitor at the book shop. Two or three times a week at least he would come in the morning and leave his cloth bag for the day while he went about on his lecturing or other literary or journalistic affairs. He was a great man to pump for information. Colonel Higginson once said of him to me, "Mr. Sanborn has the most encyclopedic mind I have ever known and one of the most inaccurate." I recall an amusing incident when Mr. Morgan was in the store one day looking at some Audubon prints. Sanborn dropped in, and, as was his wont, entered into the conversation. Turning aside for a moment to examine a folio volume of Piranesi, he remarked, "What have we here?" and, glancing over the fine Roman views, "Oh," he said, "this is Piranesi," to which Mr. Morgan remarked casually that he had a complete set of Piranesi's work. Sanborn, with lifted eyebrows, remarked in a superior tone, "Indeed, do you know that they are very rare?" Mr. Morgan replied that he believed that complete sets were somewhat scarce, and the conversation ended, neither party knowing the identity of the other. Considering Mr. Sanborn's journalistic attitude towards capitalists in general, I have no doubt he would have been chagrined had he known to whom he was speaking.

I had not been open many weeks before my interest in early American engraving was started. It was occasioned by the fact that there was a little local group who were keenly interested in this form of American art. Some were collectors of the delicate steel plates engraved by John Cheney for *The Token*, *The Gift*, and other annuals; others were interested in the work of early engravers, such as David Edwin, some of whose stippled engravings have considerable merit; but of course the more serious collectors were concerned with the important prints by Revere, Doolittle, Norman, and others whose work had little artistic but very much historical and antiquarian importance. Some were also keen collectors of early American bookplates. One of these collectors was Dr. Charles E. Clark, a physician of Lynn. Dr. Clark was my best customer at the time. He was a liberal buyer, a very generous man, and an indefatigable hunter. He haunted book shops, auction rooms, secondhand furniture dealers, and was not averse to keeping in touch with junk shops, where at times marvelous finds were made. One day Dr. Clark came in and I showed him a small Boston edition of *Josephus* with its copperplate frontispieces engraved by Amos Doolittle. "Doctor," I said, "I think you asked for Doolittle engravings and here are some." "No," he said, "it must have been James Terry of Hartford." "You are wrong," I said. "If it was not you, it was _____." "Oh," he exclaimed, "_____ wants them, does he? Well, he can't have them," and dropped the set into his bag. "Charge them to me." It seems that there was a collectors' feud between the two men, occasioned by a personal quarrel, which I do not need to relate here. This reminds me of a similar tale of George D. Smith, then the principal American dealer in rare books, whom many of us remember as the man who set the pace on high prices for rare books in New York. The story goes that one day one of Smith's clerks was at an unimportant sale at the Anderson Galleries when his boss dropped in. Smith paid little attention to the proceedings until a volume of no particular importance, but of some rarity, was put up. To everybody's surprise the book, which was started at a few cents, was carried up to something over $100, at which price Mr. Smith became the owner. Later in the afternoon his assistant said to him, "What did you want of that book that you bought at Anderson's? It isn't worth anything, is it?" "No," Smith replied, "and I didn't want it, but so-and-so" (mentioning a collector with whom Smith was at odds) "did want it, and here goes." With that he tore the volume into several pieces, which he threw into the wastebasket.

Speaking of junk-store finds reminds me of the experience of

Mr. Z. T. Hollingsworth, whose magnificent collection of Washington prints I am glad to say is still owned by his sons. Mr. Hollingsworth collected a fine set of the autographs of the signers of the Declaration of Independence. One day a friend called at his office and said, "Here, Hollingsworth, I understand that you are interested in old autographs. I was going through Charlestown to-day and passing near the Navy Yard I saw an old ash barrel on the sidewalk with some papers sticking out. Here is one which looked interesting and I pulled it out. Perhaps you would like it." This gift was an autograph document in the hand of Elbridge Gerry, dated Philadelphia, July 9, 1776. The contents were of no importance, but it was not only written by Gerry, one of the signers of the Declaration, but was also autographed by all the other Massachusetts "signers," including John Hancock, Samuel Adams, John Adams, and Robert Treat Paine. When Mr. Hollingsworth's autographs were sold at auction in 1927, this document was knocked down to me at $1,850.

Mr. Hollingsworth was a man for whom we all had the highest regard both as a man and as a collector. One of my earliest purchases of rare American prints was the excessively rare mezzotint engravings of George and Martha Washington described in No. 1 in Hart's *Catalogue of Washington Portraits*, published by the Grolier Club. When I bought these prints I knew little, if anything, about engravings or their makers, but these mezzotints appealed to me very strongly for their antiquarian value and I became greatly interested in them. They were brought to me by an antique-furniture dealer who, having promised to sell them to me, came in to say that he was sending them to New York. "But," I said, "I thought you were going to let me have them." "Oh yes, I know it," he replied; "you can have them, but I don't believe you would want to pay the price which I want for them. You see, I have heard of a concern in New York named Kennedy, who sell prints and I think they will pay me a lot for them, so I am going to send them on to them. I think that's a concern that you ought to know, because you might do some business with them."

A price was then named which I thought I could pay, and I bought them. After some mental trial essays on fixing a price, I decided to ask $1,000 for the pair. Declining an offer of $500, and irritating another collector who wanted them but thought the price was excessive, I decided to take them to New York myself, as I wanted to turn them into cash. The day before I planned to go, however, someone gave me Mr. Hollingsworth's name and suggested I write to him about them. I did so and he came in the next morning. He was very much interested. When I told him the price, he said, "No, I will not give it. If I was sure that I should never have another chance to get those prints, I would pay it gladly, but I have been collecting Washington prints since I was twenty-five years old; I am now fifty-three, and in all that time I have never seen so many rare Washington prints come into the market as within the last five years. At the price you ask I think I will wait and take my chance." More conversation followed, and I reduced the price to $900. Mr. Hollingsworth advanced his first offer of $750 to $800, and there we parted. Before leaving, however, he said, "Are you willing to let me think the matter over till to-morrow?" Of course I acquiesced and eagerly looked for him the next forenoon. He did not come in, but about two o'clock a messenger came with a note, the wording of which I remember very well to-day: "Dear Mr. Goodspeed, If you feel inclined to take $50 less than the price you named yesterday for the two prints, the bearer will hand you a check for the amount. If not, I trust you will bear me in mind when any other good things in my line come your way." That letter settled the transaction and fixed my opinion of Mr. Hollingsworth, not only as a liberal buyer but as a man of a fine spirit.

Other collectors in the same line as Mr. Hollingsworth were George R. Barrett of Boston, W. F. Havemeyer of New York, and Clarence S. Bement, Hampton L. Carson, and the Honorable John T. Mitchell of Philadelphia. All of these were eager collectors of American engraved portraits, particularly those of Washington, and they kept the prices of rarities at a very comfortable altitude.

Mention of Mr. Bement recalls to my mind an incident which happened after he had sold his collection of Washingtoniana and was interested in early engraved colonial currency. Calling at the store one day and looking over a box of odds and ends of such pieces, he asked my price for a small lot, on which I knew of no real market value. The price I named was satisfactory, but of an other piece, which he held out from the rest, he said, "And how much for this?" Thinking that it must be of some particular value, I said at a guess, "Would $5 be satisfactory?" He replied, "If it is to you, it is to me. Suppose we say $15, which I should be glad to pay for it."

I have had many trifling but pleasant incidents of this kind, another of which I might mention. When Maude Adams was putting on the spectacle of *Joan of Arc* at the stadium in Cambridge, her secretary came in one day when rehearsals were on, saying, "Miss Adams is very anxious to get some old French prints of military maneuvers showing the handling of troops." By chance I had a small lot of small folio engravings, which, while not quite of the period, appeared to be sufficiently early to answer Miss Adams's needs. Her secretary took these on approval and promised to make a report on them, but failed to do so. Miss Adams left town and I heard nothing more from them. At first I thought of dropping the matter, but finally decided to make a nominal charge of $3, the prints having no particular commercial value. That was in the spring. I heard nothing more from them until autumn, when a letter came from Miss Adams's business agent, in which she said that Miss Adams had received my bill for the prints but that she did not agree with me in my estimate of their value and enclosed a check for $20. If collectors occasionally benefit by an accidental bargain, the dealer profits as well. Few collectors can resist the temptation to boast under such circumstances and thus give due return to the seller in advertising. This, however, is not always the case, and in one instance at least the low price on a book benefited only the various dealers through whose hands it passed before reaching one who had become a good customer and who came to me with: "Congratulate me! I have just secured the only known presentation copy of the first edition of *Tom Sawyer.* How much do you think I paid for it?" My reply hazarded a guess well up in four figures, and his answer indicated that the guess came close to the mark. "I am glad you got it," I said. "That book interests me, particularly as I sold it from my Catalogue No. 74 in 1909 for $10."

> 68 **Clemens.** Adventures of Tom Sawyer. Clo., 6½x8⅜. Hartford, 1876. $10.00
> * FIRST EDITION.
> ** PRESENTATION COPY, with inscription on fly-leaf: "To C. W. Stoddard, from his friend, S. L. CLEMENS, 1877."

Lest this price should reflect on my judgment of values, I may add that although several thousand copies of this catalogue were distributed to collectors and to all the principal booksellers I had but three orders for the book, amazing as the price seems to-day.

Andrew Lang, in discussing book-buying ethics, once asked, "Is the buyer ever justified in taking advantage of the ignorance of a bookseller? I don't know, for I never had the chance." My feeling has always been that, in the dealings between collector and bookseller, the collector is entitled to any bargains he can get. It is the business of the dealer to know his stock, as he has ample opportunities of informing himself. Between the dealer and a private owner the case is quite different, and I believe that the dealer is bound to pay to an uninformed owner a price which represents a reasonable proportion of the amount he can get. Of course there are difficulties here because there are so many books which either from their rarity or from some unique feature are of uncertain value. In such cases the dealer, of course, has to protect himself and make a safe purchase, but if his sale of the piece results in an unexpected profit, should he not share it with the original owner, although under no legal obligation to do so? I remember that quite a number of years ago I was buying some books from Miss Georgiana Boutwell, the daughter of Grant's Secretary of the Treasury. There was but one book of value in the lot. At that time I was consigning a few items to a New York auction sale and included this volume, the 1702 edition of the Connecticut Acts and Laws. To my amazement it brought $1,600. Here I was in a quandary. I had bought the book believing I had paid a fair price for it, and I do not think anyone could have anticipated that it would have possibly brought such a price in those days. What should I do? I finally decided to put the whole case before Miss Boutwell and get her view of the situation. She, quite to my satisfaction, referred me to her lawyer, who, with a quizzical smile on his face as I told him the circumstances, said, "Well, what do you propose?" I replied, "Well, I don't know what you think about it, but supposing that I were to divide with Miss Boutwell the extra amount realized. Do you think this would be satisfactory?" He agreed that it would be.

Possibly the prices on some of the more important items in those early catalogues may be of interest to-day.

In our Catalogue No. 5 of January, 1901, I find "Whitman, Walt. Holograph MS. Biographical Sketch of William Douglas O'Connor. 14 pp. Neatly mounted. With the manuscript is a printer's proof corrected by Whitman, with additional instructions and request for another proof, $17.50." In the previous catalogue an original manuscript of Whitman's "After All Not to Create Only," written on twenty-eight sheets "with numerous changes, additions, eliminations, and alterations" was priced at $100. A choice copy of the first edition of Longfellow's *The Spanish Student* in the original binding, with a presentation inscription from Longfellow, was valued at $35. But I think that the prize offering of the period by Goodspeed's was in Catalogue No. 6 (April, 1901), where an immaculate copy of the first edition of Emerson's *Nature*, with a presentation inscription from Thoreau incorporating a quotation from Burns, was priced at $100. Mr. Wakeman bought this volume and it seems to have been one of the bargains at the sale of his library twenty-three years later, when it realized only $160. In the same year I find we offered what was probably our first copy of Paul Revere's engraving of the "Boston Massacre" for $650. The French copy had just been sold at auction for $800. I suppose that, in all, we must have had from twelve to fif-

143

teen copies of this much sought for, although not particularly rare, print. The crude quaintness, historical significance, and fame of the engraver (greatly enhanced by Longfellow's famous verses) sustain the demand for this engraving, although its value has not greatly appreciated in the last thirty years.

I recall an interesting experience connected with the purchase of one of these prints at a later date. A copy not in the best of condition was brought in to me one morning by a stranger from Hartford, Connecticut, a man of middle age who was by trade a decorator. After some demur my offer based on its condition was accepted. About that time I had an inquiry from Dr. Rosenbach for Revere's "Boston Massacre" and I sent this to him on approval. A fortnight or so having elapsed, the man from whom I had bought it appeared one morning in a perturbed state of mind. He gave me the history of the print as follows: It was during the War and he had undertaken the sale to druggists of a lot of absorbent cotton owned by an auctioneer. Being short of money for travelling expenses, and seeing this print in the auctioneer's office, the vendor told him that if he could sell it he could apply the proceeds to his expense account. On the basis of this agreement, he spoke to me concerning the print, and not finding the auctioneer in when he returned to get it, took it from the wall and brought it to me. After making this statement he said, "Now, Mr. Goodspeed, this fellow denies the agreement, says that I took the print without authority, and has had me arrested for larceny." "When does the case come up?" I said. He replied that he was to be in court that morning. Of course there was nothing for me to do but to go down and see the thing through. It was just a clear-cut case of two parties denying *in toto* the statements made by the other. One was lying. Which one was it? I think the judge was a little puzzled, and his decision bears out that thought. He found my man guilty, but put him on probation. This left me in the embarrassing position of having purchased, sold, and delivered a print to which I had no title. I, therefore, wrote to Dr. Rosenbach, explaining the circumstances, and he very kindly saw me out of the dilemma by returning it. I then notified the legal owner to call for the print, but he failed to do so and, after various reminders, about six months later he said to me, "Why don't you buy the print of me? You'll never get anything out of the man from whom you bought it and perhaps you can make a profit on it and reimburse yourself." He was wrong in this, however, because I had already been repaid about two-thirds of the purchase price. However, I said, "Yes, I will buy it and I will give you just what I gave for it before." This offer he accepted and it became my property without having left the premises.

Thirty years ago dealers like Mr. Foley and myself purchased a good deal of material from scouts who roamed the country within fifty miles of Boston, searching for books, pamphlets, broadsides, and most of all for early American engravings, which, as I have said, were then much in demand. Some of these scouts were interesting characters, although not always trustworthy. One of them, a short, round-faced, jolly chap, was notoriously given to romancing. One never knew whether to take the statements of his finds seriously until he produced the goods, but he did get enough good material to make it unsafe to act upon the distrust which we all had of his veracity. The following indicates a typical interview. "Oh Mr. Goodspeed, you know that old house out on the Wilmington Road near Billerica. It's a long, clapboarded, story-and-a-half building that used to be a tavern way back in the Revolutionary days. Well, that building has been closed for fifty years. When the man who owned it died he had two young sons and they had a row over the estate. They couldn't agree and the building has been closed all these years. Now both brothers are dead and the heirs asked me to go out and look over the stuff. Up in the second story there is a room which is just filled with broadsides and almanacs and primers and old schoolbooks and Revolutionary pamphlets and old pictures, and—well, you never saw anything like it in your life." This would all be pure imagination. Another morning—"Oh Mr. Goodspeed, I went out to church last night. I don't go to church very often, but my wife got me to go out to the Congregational Church and when the minister got up he said,

'I am going to talk about something that has been suggested to me by the motto that Mr. Goodspeed has over that book shop of his down on Park Street in Boston, *Anything that's a book*,' and my wife nudged me and she said, 'How much do you suppose Goodspeed paid him for that?'" Pure fiction! And another time, knowing that I was in search of a certain very rare Washington engraving, he came in and described a house in a small town in southern New Hampshire just over the Massachusetts line, where he had seen that print. He assured me that the engraving could be purchased and described the house, its location on the street, and suggested that I go to look at it. It was only after I had actually made two trips, the second following a further explanation of the locality, that I awoke to the fact that I had been chasing a "ghost" mezzotint. But this man did get things of value. He once brought me the very rare folio engraving by Doolittle of Washington surrounded by the arms of the thirteen states, pasted on the inside of a trunk cover.

Of course, I have had to do scouting myself, and at times I have made important finds in the shops of secondhand dealers in outlying districts. I remember once calling upon a venerable, long-bearded eccentric in New Bedford. His small shop was in two sections, the front for the public and the rear a sanctum sanctorum from which the public was excluded. Just how it happened I never knew, but when I called upon him, after a little talk, he did allow me to enter this room, from which I carried off a lot of unusual things, the most interesting being an anonymous *History of the British Dominions in North America*, printed in London, in 1773. This was formerly owned by Josiah Quincy, contained his bookplate, and had the following note on the flyleaf in his hand: "Purchased in Philadelphia out of the library of Benj. Franklin. The notes marked with red ink, were probably memoranda made by himself. J. Q." Some of these notes are long and of unusual interest. The volume is now in the Boston Public Library.

Prints and autographs have been included in our business from the start. Collecting autographs I have always thought to be one of the most fascinating of hobbies for any one with a taste for literature or history, if for no other reason than that no two collections are alike, every autograph letter or document being different in some respect from any other, and of course the interest and value of individual specimens vary tremendously with the importance of the contents of the specimen. Three autographs which I recall are especially noteworthy and perhaps the best pieces which I have had in this department. The first was one of the very few copies which Franklin made of his famous *Epitaph*: "The Body of Benjamin Franklin, Printer, (like the cover of an old book, its contents torn out, and stript of its lettering and gilding) lies here, food for worms. But the work shall not be lost, for it will, as he believed, appear once more, in a new and more elegant edition, revised and corrected, by The Author." The second autograph which I have in mind, and which must be of excessive rarity, was a letter from Mary Washington to "My son Georg," and the last of the three a full autograph letter signed from Martha Washington to Mrs. John Adams, acknowledging Mrs. Adams's letter of condolence upon the death of her husband. The Franklin document was bought from the family of a descendent of Colonel Thomas Aspinwall, a well-known Bostonian, who was United States consul at London a century or so ago. This manuscript was sold to Dr. Rosenbach, who mentions it in *Books and Bidders*. The Mary Washington letter was bought at Libbie's Auction Room in 1912. The owner stated at the time that it was bought by him from the Desforges collection, which was dispersed by Sullivan Brothers and Libbie in 1881. I remember sitting beside Mr. Walter R. Benjamin at the sale and saying to him, "What do you think of this autograph of Mary Washington?" He replied rather nervously, "I don't know, I never saw one before. I have an order on it, but I don't know what to bid." The letter had been folded in three places, and had been damaged by fire along the folds, but the date, "Martch the 13 1782," and the subscription, "Loveing and affectinat Mother, Mary Washington," were intact. Possibly Mr. Benjamin had some doubts about its genuineness, for he dropped out when the bidding

147

reached $250, at which price I purchased it. It is now in the Morgan collection.

I once received a letter from a woman living in Washington, saying that she had amongst the papers of her late husband, who had been the chief clerk in one of the departments of Washington, a collection of documents signed by several of the presidents, which she would like to sell and of which she gave a general description, with a price on the lot. I asked her to send them to me and when I got them I was in such a hurry to accept her offer that I sent her the check by return mail, but upon thinking it over, I began to have some doubts as to whether they had been acquired by her husband properly. The autographs were of presidents from Tyler down to Lincoln and were all signed to an identical lithographed form, which read as follows: "I hereby authorize and direct the Secretary of State to affix the seal of the United States to (_____) Dated this day, and signed by me and for so doing this shall be his warrant. Washington _____." Here followed the signature of the president, with the date, and in the blank above there was written a description of the document to which the authorization referred. It looked as though these documents might have been abstracted from Government files. I therefore wrote immediately to the lady, expressing my doubts and asking her not to consider the transaction closed until she could assure me of her right to their ownership, and that to decide this I would, with her permission, write to the Secretary of State for information. On her assent I made the inquiry, to which Secretary Root replied to the effect that he had investigated the matter and found that these documents were part of a lot which, being regarded as of no further value, had been removed from the Government Archives to be destroyed during the second Cleveland administration. He added (presumably for its effect upon department officials) that although the Government did not regard it as necessary to take any action concerning these papers under the circumstances, any future sale of documents which had been marked for destruction would be severely punished. Apart from the presidential signatures, the interest in these papers was of course in their association with the proclamations to which they referred. One of those signed by Lincoln, for example, authorized the fixing of the seal to "My proclamation appointing a day of humiliation, prayer and fasting (12th August 1861)." Another, signed by Polk, referred to his "Proclamation of War with the Republic of Mexico."

Three peculiar dangers beset the bookseller, and from these he has little protection save his own honesty, good judgment, and alertness. First is the danger of buying material which has been stolen either from individuals or, more often, from public libraries, and to avoid this danger he must always be on his guard. He is also, from the nature of his merchandise, in constant peril from sneak thieves. He cannot set a watch upon visitors without giving offence, and culprits when caught seldom receive punishment. The courts for some reason are lenient in such cases, and the offender usually gets off with probation or a filed case. The third danger is from the forger. There are forgers of books, forgers of prints, forgers of autographs, indeed fakers of almost everything antiquarian which has a value. A book in which a dozen or so booksellers might contribute a chapter from their own personal experience with these pitfalls would be readable.

My first experience with a forger was with a Philadelphian, whose adventures from Canada to South Carolina are now famous, and who victimized nearly every American dealer of prominence. Another forger, whose identity so far as I know has never been discovered, presented his wares so cleverly that he found easy victims. (Incidentally I might remark that after many bitter experiences I have learned to abide by first impressions. Many times I have been just a little suspicious of a document, but finally convinced myself that it was genuine, only to discover in the end that my first judgment was the correct one. If one has any intuition in such matters, I think he will discover this a safe rule to follow.) The forger I speak of called upon me about twenty-five years ago. I see, however, that I am getting a little ahead of my story. About two years previous to this call a woman brought in two Rowlandson drawings. At least she said they were drawn by Rowlandson, and I have no doubt that they were, as they were characteristic of his manner, well executed in water color. I was not handling drawings, I did not know anything about them, and I made no offer. Going back to the beginning of the story, the caller whom I have mentioned was a middle-aged Englishman, of the cockney type. The tale he told me was of a friend in Canada who had known of the existence of some old manuscripts for a number of years and had been trying to buy them from their owner, an old lady who had recently died, and from whose estate his friend had just purchased them. Thinking that he might find a better market in the United States, he had sent them here for sale. My cockney visitor said that he had offered them to one of the faculty at Harvard College, who referred him to the Bostonian Society, where in turn he had been sent to Mr. Charles H. Taylor, Jr., of the *Boston Globe*, who now passed him on to me. Of course I should have known that someone of this group would have been interested in buying these very important documents before they got to me. However, I was so much taken with the lot that this obvious fact escaped me. Neither did I take warning from the suspiciously low price at which the lot was offered. Here were several (as I recall it, seven or eight) drawings in pen and ink, about 4" x 6" in size, of American forts, and a plan of lower New York of about the same dimensions. The latter bore the date of October 2, 1780, and the initials "H. C." On the lower corner of the map was the signature "Jno. André, Dept. Adt. Genl." On the margins of some of the plans were figures separated by dots, which appeared to indicate a cipher reference. With these documents were a few relics, an old iron inkwell with the initials "J. A." rudely scratched on its side, a parchment tobacco pouch with "Jno. André, 23rd Foot Hounslow" in ink along its neck, and a delicate cameo locket set with turquoises and pendant from a fine old gold chain. The price of the lot was $65. After making the purchase I made some remark about André, and the seller (with a finesse common in such transactions) professed to be ignorant of the historical interest and value of this material, and added, "I've also got an old drinking song, which perhaps had something to do with these things." This aroused my curiosity and the next day he brought it in. The "drinking song" was a pocket edition of Churchill's poems, in which a convivial song was the first piece printed. The interesting part of this little volume, however, was in the figures which were written on the inside of the covers. They were very much like the figures which appeared upon the manuscript plans, and in the text of the book various letters or words were underlined, the whole indicating a cipher and possibly a key to the figures on the plans. (More finesse.) This was a tremendous find, and my next catalogue was to have reproductions of all of these intensely interesting manuscripts. I did go to the precaution of sending the map of New York (and, by the way, some of the plans also had André's name or initials on them) to an institution which owned several André letters for their opinion concerning the genuineness of the signature. The unofficial reply I received from them was favorable. They indeed expressed an opinion that the initials "H. C." were surely in Sir Henry Clinton's hand.

Having, therefore, not the slightest suspicion that the material was not perfectly good, I was, as I said, about to go forward with the marketing of them when I had a call from Frank Coburn, a dealer at whose shop in Cornhill I made frequent purchases. He said, "I want you to come down to my store and look at some Revolutionary caricatures which have been left with me on sale. They are very curious and interesting. They are colored." I put on my hat and went down to Cornhill with him, where I received the shock of my life when I found that there were the two Rowlandson drawings which had been offered to me about two years before. At that time they were unlettered. Now each one of them had a caption converting them into "Revolutionary caricatures." I will describe one of them. It represented the interior of a tavern, with three or four figures. One of these was of a man seated, reaching into his trousers' pocket, presumably for his wallet to liquidate the landlady's bill. The landlady was standing in front, holding her bill before him, while his companion was chucking her under the chin with his hand. As I have said, I

151

have no doubt this was a genuine Rowlandson drawing, a character-istic tavern scene. How could this be titled to make it a "Revolutionary caricature"? The answer shows how clever a party we were dealing with. It read: "The British after a brief sojourn prepare to leave Boston. Madame Boston presents her bill for accommodation." Upon my explaining the status of the drawings Coburn's natural query was, "What makes you think that this picture is not genuine?" I replied, "I am sure the picture *is* genuine, but I also know that the title has been added very recently." "Do you mean to say," he replied, "that that is not old writing? See how brown the ink is." "Yes," I answered, "the ink is undoubtedly brown, but the writing is quite modern for all of that. What about the mat around the picture?" "Oh, of course that is a modern mat." I then with a penknife lifted the inside margin of the mat showing that not a single loop letter projected below, satisfying him that the writing was later than the mat. The writing also appeared to be identical with that on my Revolutionary plans. This, with some other suspicious circumstances, assured me that the locket and the antique inkwell were all that there was of value in my purchase, a conclusion which I shall have to ask the reader to accept without going into lengthy details.

This "André" lot remained in my hands for some time. One day the late William Loring Andrews of New York, on looking it over, questioned my judgment in condemning the material. When I related the whole circumstances, however, he had to admit that I was right. "But," he added, "I never saw that map of New York before, and it is just the kind of map which I am looking for to illustrate the book which I am writing on *New York as Washington Knew it at the Close of the Revolution.* I should like to use it in my book." "Very well," I said, "you are quite at liberty to do so, and I shall make no charge for its use for that purpose, but I want you to understand very clearly what my opinion of it is." With that understanding he took it to Sidney L. Smith, who engraved it very beautifully. Those curious in such matters will find the plate published in the book to which I have referred.

About this time other forgeries appeared in the market. In Libbie's Auction Room there was offered a silhouette portrait of George Walton, signer of the Declaration of Independence, with an alleged presentation inscription to Button Gwinnett; a Boston dealer bought an anonymous one-volume *History of England*, published in London about 1765, with the inscription: "To honoured uncle from his obliged servant Oliver Goldsmith"; while another exhibited a piece of sheet music on which was inscribed: "Mrs. Custis from G. W." I suggested that before offering it for sale, it might be well to find out when the song was written. As I recall it now the date was some twenty years subsequent to that of the autograph presentation! All these and some other specimens which have appeared intermittently ever since seem to have been produced by the same person, whose identity, I believe, has not been discovered.

I might ramble on but the space assigned to me here is used up and I bring this random reminiscence to a close, with feelings akin to those of the garrulous speaker as the crash of the gavel strikes on his ear. After all, it is of the sort which describes the daily routine of most booksellers, and, like one's offspring, is probably of slight interest to others. Nevertheless it may serve to give a personal note to this catalogue, which aims to present a cross section of the various departments of our stock to all our customers, of whom many are on our list only for certain special subjects. It is a pleasure for me to know that this catalogue has been printed by The Merrymount Press, with which I have had gratifying business relations for more than thirty years. If Catalogue 250 should in any way increase our most valuable asset—the good will of our customers—we shall be repaid for our labor in its preparation.

CHARLES E. GOODSPEED

October 30, 1935

Appendix B

Supplement to Goodspeed's Fiftieth Anniversary Catalogue
(No. 423, November 1948).

FIFTIETH
ANNIVERSARY
1898-GOODSPEED'S-1948

"Travelled a good deal in" Boston —

5A Park Street, 1898-1930 —— 7 & 9A Ashburton Place, 1921-1935
2 Milk Street, 1927-1948 —— 18 Beacon Street, 1935-1948 →

2

156

BOOK SHOP BIRTHDAY
GOODSPEED'S COMPLETES FIFTY YEARS
OF SELLING "ANYTHING THAT'S A BOOK"

As Kai Lung would say, the beginning was "at a period so remote that it would be impious to doubt whatever happened then." In November, 1898, Harvard astronomers pronounced the Leonid meteors satisfactory and the gentleman from the *Transcript* reported Harvard football to be "retrograding." McKinley was President, Teddy Roosevelt was Governor-elect of New York, and Rough Rider hats were seen on the heads of the less inhibited male Bostonians.

It was chrysanthemum time at Horticultural Hall and Captain Dreyfus was packing to leave Devil's Island. In Jerusalem Kaiser William confided, "I ring out the cry, voicing my ardent hope to all, 'Peace on earth.'" In Boston Congressman John F. Fitzgerald was reëlected, as Ward Eight groaned. "Sweet Adeline" was around the corner. Calumet & Hecla went to 521 and R. H.

3

157

PARK STREET INTERIOR—Fifty-five dollars a month, in cash, in advance.

		Ex...	Pur...	Cost	Sales	Profit
Week End Dec	10	109.85	538.68	77.84	144.10	66.26
	17	32.84	133.56	69.31	119.95	50.64
	24	1.05	148.73	108.	196.85	88.85
	31	68.25	65.34	52.65	94.67	42.02
Jan	7	28.63	11.40	88.81	152.90	64.09
	14	21.15	56.36	38.03	64.85	26.82
	21	31.03	189.93	49.31	91.58	42.27
	28	6.90	9.52	69.14	115.76	46.62
Feby	4	61.29	38.25	25.88	54.93	29.05
	11	12.	147.67	60.88	102.99	42.36
	18	24.98	56.12	63.51	106.38	42.87
	25	14.04	11.05	72.78	143.58	70.80
Mch	4	64.05	204.77	137.73	189.03	51.80
	11	17.54	164.61	82.51	134.63	57.12
	18	11.70	124.30	85.80	183.35	97.55
	25	11.50	385.54	191.49	299.57	108.08
Apr	1	65.25	327.78	252.86	325.11	72.25

BOOKKEEPING IN 1898—Now it is accomplished by wheels within wheels.

Stearns sold four-button doeskin gloves for sixty-five cents. Spanish War heroes had stopped shooting and begun talking. Proposed annexation of the Philippines was opposed by Spain, the religious press, and Aguinaldo. "We are on the brink of empire," said Senator Penrose.

A Gutenberg Bible sold for $14.750 and the best golf balls were three for a dollar. Kate Douglas Wiggin and Rudyard Kipling had best-sellers. A man named Westcott wrote a "promising" book named *David Harum* and *Mr. Dooley in Peace and War* was "just out." T. R. lectured at Lowell Institute, James

4

158

"C.E." looked like this when   Michael Walsh came to work in 1909.*

Whitcomb Riley fetched smiles and tears at Tremont Temple, and Hall Caine registered at the Touraine. DeWolf Hopper was at the Tremont in *The Charlatan*, Maude Adams at the Hollis in *The Little Minister*. And John Drew was finding Hoff's Malt Extract "very beneficial for brainworkers."

Harvard beat Yale 17-0 in the rain at New Haven and the Department of Agriculture battled to a scoreless tie with the chinch-bugs. The Boston Nationals won the league championship. Babies ate Mellin's Food and irritable oldsters downed Horsford's Acid Phosphate. Coachmen were wanted and Constant Reader wrote to ask, "Have Horseless Carriages the Rights of Vehicles?" The Lizzie Borden jury held a reunion at the Revere House, and at month's end came a heavy snowfall. Horsecars were stalled, snowshoes were seen on St. Botolph Street, and the steamer *Portland* went down.

The financial editor of the *Transcript* gloated genteelly in the radiance of "the best business year" in American history, while practising tradesmen continued to wear the worried look acquired in the Depression of 1893. Government hospitals housed yellow fever casualties and a book-trade letter of the season reported that "the end of the war came at an opportune time for autumn business." The year that began with the bang of Remember the *Maine!* ended with a simper: "What does the Dickey bird say?" Taking one thing with another, it was as good a time as any for a young farm-machinery salesman named Goodspeed to find himself out of a twenty-seven-hundred-dollar job.

Charles E. Goodspeed, transplanted Cape Codder, put the question to the proprietor of the book shop at 15 Ann Street: "Mr. Mendoza, I have lost my job in New York and am going back to Boston. What do you think of my chances in the secondhand book business?" "I never knew but one man who failed in it," Isaac Mendoza replied, "and he played the races." In Boston the same question was asked and answered at Libbie's Auction Room: "Charles, if you can get

* From a photograph taken in September 1948.

5

159

AL FRESCO—William Foley, long-time customer, riffles the fresh-air shelves before descending the fifteen steps into the Milk Street shop.

AES TRIPLEX—The first-floor vault at Beacon Street houses rare books and first editions. A *Tamerlane* here, a *Tamerlane* there—it all adds up.

6

a job at $20 a week, don't think of going into secondhand books." With a family to support, Mr. Goodspeed divided the answers by two and made his own decision.

A $55 basement shop in Park Street he stocked largely with a miscellany from Bangs's Auction Rooms and remainders from the skin-deep beautiful bankrupt stock of Stone & Kimball, picked up at Mendoza's. These, with twinges, he fortified with his own collections of Ruskin and Dr. Thomas William Parsons. Boston's newest antiquarian bookseller hopefully hovered by his denim-covered box of a desk and waited for customers who were doing their Christmas shopping early. The first day's receipts topped $20.

The one-man shop that began in the *fin de siècle* years of the Gay Nineties had, by the end of the Roaring Twenties, become a three-shop enterprise employing nearly fifty men, women, and boys. Few antiquarian book shops have ever been serviced by so large a staff, made necessary in Goodspeed's case by the scope of a big stock of books, autographs, and prints — each specialty under the hand of an expert, aided by an assistant or secretary, and the whole requiring a framing and restoring serviceman, bookkeepers, mailing clerks, shippers, errand boys, and dust engineers. Following the closing of the original Park Street shop, and in the doldrums of the Thirties, the size of the staff was reduced, but today's total personnel remains impressive as book shop staffs go. Oldest member of the staff in years of employment is Michael J. Walsh, chief of the Americana Department, who came to work in the Park Street shop in 1909. Nearly half of the present employees have been at Goodspeed's twenty years or better. In the antiquarian book world, length of experience is significant.

The story of Goodspeed's Book Shop is fully told in the proprietor's autobiography, *Yankee Bookseller* (Boston, 1937) and briefly in his preface to Goodspeed's Catalogue No. 250 (1935). During the fifty years of its existence, the sign of the Monk on Horseback has hung over four Goodspeed shops in Boston — the Park Street

BEACON STREET FIRST FLOOR AND BALCONY — Right to left, Director Walter Kahoe of J. B. Lippincott, Philadelphia; Arnold Roy of Goodspeed's framing department; Librarian Walter Whitehill of the Boston Athenaeum; Goodspeed's George Goodspeed; Alexander Novick of Beacon Hill.

original, the ample premises at 7 & 9a Ashburton Place, the prairie-wide basement of the Old South Meeting House, and, most recently, at brownstone 18 Beacon Street. At one period three of these shops were concurrent.

In 1930 the Park Street shop, of sentimental memory, was closed. The closing evoked an interest on the part of the press that was not apparent at the debut in November, 1898. The removal was preceded by a sale, at the end of which it was found that several thousand volumes remained unsold, with three days of lease to go. A poster appeared in the sidewalk-level window: "Free! Help Yourself! Every Book in This Store Given Away. No Dealers. Limit Ten Volumes or One Set to a Person."

Reporters and police were present. The evening papers reported from five to ten thousand books disposed of in two hours, ten at a time . . . "one dignified matron emerged from the shuffle . . . handed her ten books to a waiting chauffeur."

In 1936 the Ashburton Place premises were vacated, without fanfare, for the Beacon Street shop which Goodspeed's now operates, along with the Old South Branch. Into the big Beacon Street windows come rays from the golden State House dome that Dr. Oliver Wendell Holmes called the "hub of the solar system," which makes Goodspeed's the most centrally located old book shop in the universe. The Beacon Street shop houses collectors' specialties, purveyed by a staff of specialists in first editions, Americana, autographs, old prints, and books on fine arts and the crafts. It also houses the world's largest dealer's stock of American genealogy and local history. The Old South Branch at 2 Milk Street contains a diversity of secondhand and out-of-print books with virtues

7

161

THE HUB—Holmes called the State House "the hub of the solar system." Goodspeed's is located a pop-fly's flight from the cosmic center.

of their own but minus the special collector-interests of the Beacon Street stock.

Fifty years is not a long period in Cathay. Even in America it is not uncommon for a business to complete its fiftieth year, but it is uncommon anywhere for one to touch fifty with the original proprietor still at the helm. Charles E. Goodspeed is president of Goodspeed's Book Shop, Inc. In recent years he has spent more time in writing books than in selling them (*Yankee Bookseller, Angling in America, A Treasury of Fishing Stories* [editor], numerous historical papers for learned periodicals). Back in '98 he chose as his slogan "Anything that's a book!" —a bold promise in Boston. For fifty years he and his associates have sought

8

162

AULD LANG SYNE—Charles Goodspeed and Michael Walsh get
together over an unrecorded edition of *The New England Primer.*

to reflect this slogan in the catholicity of the stock. Even in today's inflation,
books may be bought three-for-a-quarter on the sidewalk—or for four figures
out of the vault.

Goodspeed's has sold its share of rarities, particularly in the fields of American
and English first editions, historical American books, early American prints, and
autographs and manuscripts of literary and historical great ones. Twice it has
sold the glamour-book, *Tamerlane,* but its character has always been distinguished
by the variety of its antiquarian fare, irrespective of rarity or price. "Anything
that's a book!"—that's what the man said.

9

163

THEY COME—New purchases are checked and priced by Manager George Tupper (*foreground*) of the Milk Street shop, with an assist from his lieutenant, Arnold Silverman.

. . . AND THEY GO—Per Ostman (*right*) has twenty years' experience packing valuable items for safe shipment. Ralph Cannell, armorial designer, paints coats of arms.

10

164

RARE BOOKS AND FIRST EDITIONS—George Goodspeed *(right)* and Frank Willson, visiting bookseller and formerly of Goodspeed's, pursue a point.

AUTOGRAPHS, BOOKS ON ARTS AND CRAFTS—These strange bed-fellows are tucked in and tumbled out by Gordon Banks, manager of this duplex department.

11

165

OLD AND MODERN PRINTS, PAINTINGS—Goodspeed's early added pictures, saw the department grow under guidance of the late Louis A. Holman. Doris Ashfield (*right*) shows customer Nancy Eaton old maps of Boston.

GENEALOGY—Librarian Francis Allen (*left*) of the Congregational Library and John Farquharson, manager of the world's largest stock of American family histories, with clerks Ellen Flatley and Marion Christensen.

12

166

AMERICANA—Manager Michael Walsh double-checks a point with Paul Seybolt, who collects the hard way (first editions of authors' first books), while the Reverend Joseph Ryan of St. John's Ecclesiastical Seminary pursues the even tenor.

MILK STREET SHOP—Clerks Frances Egan (*middle distance, facing right*) and Martha Pratt (*in while blouse*) serve noon-hour browsers. Milk Street menu—anything from Thucydides to Tom Swift, from B. Traven to Ben Jonson.

13

167

REFERENCE LIBRARY—Few book shops can match this. Rudolph Gerlach was with Libbie's before coming to Goodspeed's in 1930. Bob Topalian pursues a traditional enemy of books—dust.

MAILING ROOM—Alice Delahunt (*seated*) mothers a large mailing list, gets tons of catalogues on their way to those Very Important People, the customers.

14

168

BOOKKEEPING ROOM—Bookselling means bookkeeping. Head Bookkeeper Madeleine Bisson (*right*), May Walsh at accounting machine, Rita Donlon at files.

THE HIGHER THE FEWER—M. Starr Morash, Boston printer, drops in to study a new American type. On the ladder, Rita Donlon—at her desk, Margaret McLaughlin.

15

169

"Anything that's a book!"

"THE MONTH"—Now in its 20th year. Norman Dodge, editor, talks photo-engraving with Conant Barton.

QUARTER MILLION—250,000 letters, more or less, have been typed at Goodspeed's by Mary O'Hern.

AUTOGRAPHS—In steel files and morocco albums, much in little.

YANKEE TRADERS—The trick lies in the counter-punching.

16

Appendix C*

CHARLES ELIOT GOODSPEED 1867-1950
Michael J. Walsh

Charles Eliot Goodspeed was born at Cotuit, on Cape Cod on May 2, 1867 and died at Ayer, Massachusetts, October 31, 1950. His parents were Elliott Freeman Goodspeed and Abbie Ellen Dane, who were married in 1859. He was a direct descendant of Roger, the first of the family in this country, who was in Barnstable, Massachusetts in 1638. After an association of forty-one years with him, I can safely say that his long life was not only successful and useful, but was also thoroughly happy.

The story of his early life and many of his most interesting experiences in bookselling are given in his autobiography, the highly readable "Yankee Bookseller", published by Houghton Mifflin in 1937. Here among many others is told the story of the buying and selling of the two *Tamerlanes*, which passed through his hands.

The original Goodspeed shop was opened in a basement at 5a Park Street, opposite Boston Common in 1898. From his early days Mr. Goodspeed was an ardent book-lover, and in his travels as a young salesman for a farming implement concern, was a habitual visitor to old book shops. This meant that by the time he opened his shop, he had a modest private library, selections from which were offered for sale at his opening. From this small beginning in a basement, which was originally the kitchen in a private dwelling, grew a business that came to be internationally known and that at one time employed a staff of more than fifty.

---

* Obituary of Charles Eliot Goodspeed by Michael J. Walsh. Printed in *Antiquarian Bookman*, Vol. VII, No. 9, pp. 864-70, March 3, 1951.

With small capital, it takes vision, shrewdness, and acumen to build a successful business. Mr. Goodspeed had these qualities in abundance, but in addition was industrious and to an uncommon degree fair and just in all his dealings.

Not a little of his success can be attributed to lasting and in some cases intimate friendships formed early with influential Bostonians who were interested in book-collecting. His sterling character and business sagacity attracted men such as Harold Murdock, banker, book-collector, writer, and student. Mr. Murdock had an analytical and penetrating mind. His opinion on a rare book was invariably sound and often of great benefit to the young book-seller, especially at a time when bibliography was not as extensive as it is to-day.

Mr. Goodspeed was an expert letter-writer and cataloguer. Without academic training in writing, he was able to present facts lucidly and simply, and without frills. He believed book buyers to be the most intelligent people in the world and that they couldn't be taken in by phony descriptions. Of the 440 catalogues of books, prints, and autographs issued by the firm, most of the early issues were written by him. Besides "Yankee Bookseller", in later years he found time to write "Angling in America", and "A Treasury of Fishing Stories." A number of historical and bibliographical papers also came from his pen. With F. W. Bayley, he revised and enlarged Dunlap's "Rise and Progress of the Arts and Design in the United States". This three-volume work was published by Goodspeed's in 1918.

Besides his great knowledge of books, Mr. Goodspeed was also among the best at prints and autographs. His information on the works of Revere, Pelham, Doolittle, Norman, Romans, Savage, and other early American engravers was second to none. Probably more copies of that most famous of all American engravings, Revere's Boston Massacre passed through his hands than those of any other person. In "Yankee Bookseller" he lists what were in his opinion the five most important engravings of early American events: (1.) The

172

set of four engravings of the Battles of Lexington and Concord by Amos Doolittle. (2.) Revere's Boston Massacre. (3.) Blodgett's Battle of Lake George. (4.) The Landing of the British Troops in Boston in 1768 by Paul Revere. (5.) The Battle of Bunker Hill by Bernard Romans. In his time he had them all. The Doolittle engravings and Revere's Landing of the Troops are excessively rare. He also had one of the two known copies of Cyprian Southack's map of New England, Boston, 1717, which is so rare as to be unrecorded in bibliographies and which has the distinction of being the first separate American map. Like so many of the treasures which he owned, this is now at the John Carter Brown Library.

He was probably among the first to see the individual Audubon folio bird prints as fine merchandise. Many incomplete or partial sets of this great work were purchased by him to be broken up. Sometimes the number of prints in stock would run into the thousands. It is probable that he also sold at least a half dozen complete sets of the four volumes.

He became an expert on autographs long before the modern microscope, the ultra violet ray and other scientific means were used to detect forgeries. He could spot a Robert Spring forgery across the room and more than once when fake Button Gwinnett and Thomas Lynch autographs with very plausible stories behind them were offered for sale, it didn't take Mr. Goodspeed long to determine what they really were.

Shortly after he was established, Mr. Goodspeed noted the demand for genealogical books and in time built up a large stock on this subject. In 1915 with the purchase of the stock of George E. Littlefield, Cornhill bookseller, who had been a specialist in the subject, Goodspeed's became the great source of supply of books containing genealogical information. The firm has issued twenty-two catalogues on this subject alone, the last containing nearly six thousand titles.

An active bookselling career that spanned fifty years would almost of necessity include many highlights. Space forbids the mentioning of but two. These would be the purchase in 1926 of the Sumner Hollingsworth library, and in 1941 of the Matt B. Jones library. Both of these fine collections of Americana were for the most part restricted to rarities and contained many outstanding books, principally relating to early New England. The highspot in the Hollingsworth collection was John Winthrop's "A Declaration of Former Passages and Proceedings Betwixt the English and the Narrowgansets," Cambridge, printed by Stephen Daye, 1645, the first historical book printed in what is now the United States. This is still one of only four known copies, and is now at the John Carter Brown Library. The Matt B. Jones collection was justly renowned for the very fine condition of nearly all of the more than two thousand choice items. A feature of the Jones library was the owner's catalogue, neatly written on 8 by 5 inch cards. This expert job was a joy for a bookseller to behold, containing as it did all the vital information relating to the book in question, including subject matter, auction records, location of other known copies, the date of purchase, the price, and from whom it was bought. Both of these collections rank among the best in their field.

All of his prominent Boston contemporaries passed on before he did—the two Libbies, father and son; the two Lauriats, father and son; P. K. Foley; Andrew McCance; Richard Lichtenstein; N. J. Bartlett; George E. Littlefield; and George Humphry. He had most cordial relations with all of them, being particularly close to Mr. McCance whose company he thoroughly enjoyed. For a great many years they lunched together. Besides being a good book man McCance was an expert story-teller and it was a rare day when he couldn't come up with a new one. He seemed to have an inexhaustible supply.

Mr. Goodspeed was a great admirer of Foley, for the latter's great knowledge of the writings of American authors, especially the New Englanders. Both men were very generous in giving out free information, which had taken long time and effort to acquire, although

Foley wasn't bashful when it came to turning down someone he didn't particularly care about.

During his active years, Mr. Goodspeed formed the acquaintance of many famous people, who also happened to be collectors. Among them were: J. P. Morgan (the younger), Sir William Osler, Franklin D. Roosevelt, Owen D. Young, Thomas Wentworth Higginson, Gen. Nelson A. Miles, Charles Follen Adams, Thomas Nelson Page, George E. Woodberry, Robert W. Chambers, Samuel McChord Crothers, John Drinkwater, W. D. Howells, Albert J. Beveridge, Basil King, Maude Adams, Gamaliel Bradford, Childe Hassam, John Burroughs, Henry Ford, John Kendrick Bangs, Amy Lowell, Margaret Deland, Fritz Kreisler, Joseph C. Lincoln, Thomas W. Lawson, Theodore N. Vail, Laura E. Richards, Harry Houdini, and Rudolph Valentino.

Among others who owed their fame principally to collecting and who came to Goodspeed's were Daniel B. Fearing, the great angling collector; Evert Jansen Wendell; the three Hollingsworth brothers, Amor, Sumner, and Zachary; Bishop John F. Hurst; William G. Mather; Dr. William C. Braislin; Mr. and Mrs. Philip A. Rollins; Matt B. Jones; Frank C. Deering; William L. Clements; Frank Bemis; Harold Murdock; Frederick L. and Ernest Gay; W. P. Shillaber; and Dr. Samuel A. Green. The last served a term as mayor of Boston and was librarian of the Massachusetts Historical Society for fifty years.

Among collectors active at the present time, he was on intimate terms with Thomas W. Streeter, J. K. Lilly, Jr., and Parkman D. Howe.

Mr. Goodspeed's diversions outside of business were fishing, golf, and raising flowers, with a particular liking for the unusual in irises. His personal tastes in book-collecting ran to angling, American juveniles, John Ruskin, and Thomas W. Parsons. His Ruskin Collection, probably the most complete in existence, was given to Wellesley College Library.

To round out a colorful life, he received in 1935 an honorary degree from Brown University and later Phi Beta Kappa gave him honorary membership. He also served a term as president of the Colonial Society of Massachusetts, and was a former treasurer of the Bibliographical Society of America. He was an honorary fellow of the American Booksellers Association, a member of the Grolier Club, Club of Odd Volumes, Massachusetts Historical Society, American Antiquarian Society, and a number of other organizations.

He is survived by his widow, Mrs. Leila M. Goodspeed and by three children, George T. Goodspeed, who carries on the business, Mrs. Wellen H. Colburn, and Mrs. Gordon T. Banks.

Appendix D

Goodspeed's at No. 7 Beacon Street, 1981-1993 (three photographs).

By permission of the Houghton Library, Harvard University

The Autograph department

By permission of the Houghton Library, Harvard University

The Americana department (Bailey Bishop in foreground)

By permission of the Houghton Library, Harvard University

Stopping by Goodspeed's on a snowy evening

Acknowledgments

The publisher wishes to thank the following individuals and institutions for their help in preparing this book for publication: Hugh Amory; Vincent Giroud, Curator of Modern Books and Manuscripts, Beinecke Library, Yale University; Kenneth Gloss, Brattle Book Shop; George Talbot Goodspeed; James N. Green, Assistant Librarian, Library Company of Philadelphia; Barbara Ware Holmes; Sarah Anne Holmes; Patricia A. Maurer, Librarian, The Bostonian Society; Samuel R. Morrill, Edward Morrill & Son; Leslie Morris, Houghton Library, Harvard University; Ellis H. Neel, Jr.; Karen Nipps, Curator of Printed Books, Library Company of Philadelphia; Roger L. Rainwater, Coordinator for Special Collections, William Luther Lewis Collection, Mary Couts Bernett Library, Texas Christian University; Catharina Slautterback, Assistant Curator, Print Room, Library of the Boston Athanaeum; Carol Goodspeed Smith; Peter Stern, Pepper & Stern Rare Books; Roger E. Stoddard, Houghton Library, Harvard University; Stephen Weissman, Ximenes Rare Books Inc.; Clarence Wolf, Geo. S. MacManus Co.